SUMMONING
DELIVERANCE

APRIL D. MIRANDA

conversations from my memories of them. In order to maintain their anonymity in some instances, I have changed the names of individuals and places and I may have changed some identifying characteristics and details such as physical properties, occupations and places of residence.

Dedication

I dedicate this book to everyone desperate for God's will in their lives. To all those souls who have experienced the backslidden paths, may you trust God's Word to be a light unto your path and allow Him to direct your steps.

"For You have delivered my soul from death. Have You not kept my feet from falling, That I may walk before God In the light of the living?"

Psalms 56:13 NKJV

Acknowledgments

Sincerest thanks to Tiffany Buckner with Anointed Fire House for helping in the editing and publishing of this book. Heartfelt gratitude to my dear friend, Carolina, for listening to me rant daily about writing this book and finishing it in record timing. Your friendship is priceless.

Most importantly, an unlimited amount of appreciation and love to my husband, Art, and our daughters, Luna and Noah, for their earnest support. I had many restless days and sleepless nights while I pushed to finish this book. My family is my legacy.

Table of Contents

Introduction...XI

Chapter 1...

The Beginning..1

Chapter 2...

Meeting God..25

Chapter 3...

The Craft...39

Chapter 4...

Familiar Spirits and Generational Curses....51

Chapter 5...

Demonized..59

Chapter 6...

Michael, the Archangel.............................69

Chapter 7...

Renunciation..77

Chapter 8...

The Pre-Game...83

Chapter 9...

Deliverance..105

Chapter 10...

Maintaining Deliverance.........................113

Chapter 11...

Healing Within Deliverance.....................141

Chapter 12...

    God's Purpose...161

Chapter 13...

    Prayers...179

Chapter 14...

    Eyewitness Testimony................................193

Introduction

sum·mon

/ˈsəmən/

verb

gerund or present participle: summoning

1. authoritatively or urgently call on (some-one) to be present, especially as a de-fendant or witness in a law court.

de·liv·er·ance

/dəˈliv(ə)rəns/

noun

noun: deliverance; plural noun: deliver-ances

1. the action of being rescued or set free.
"prayers for deliverance"

"Beware lest anyone cheat you through philosophy and empty deceit, according to the tradition of men, according to the basic principles of the word, and not according to

Christ."

Colossians 2:8 NKJV

"Don't let anyone capture you with empty philosophies and high-sounding nonsense that comes from human thinking and from the spiritual powers of this world, rather than from Christ."

Colossians 2:8 NLT

My name is April Miranda. I am 41 years old and married with two children. On April 4, 2018, I experienced the most intense deliverance of my life in a church in New Braunfels, Texas. In an instant, I was completely delivered from the occult as well as years of demonic oppression, depression, anxiety and suicide. Nevertheless, the path leading to this moment was long and turbulent. This journey started before I was born. Generational curses and familiar spirits tried to write my life's story, but God had other plans. I was born for such a time as this.

I'd like to tell you what happened, as prompted by Holy Spirit.

Father, in the name of Jesus, I pray it be Your words which flow forth from my mind to my fingers as I type out this testimony. Bring it to completion in Your perfect will, in Jesus' name. Amen.

"But I will sing of Your power; Yes, I will sing aloud of Your mercy in the morning; For You have been my defense And refuge in the day of my trouble."

Psalms 59:16 NKJV

I am not worthy, but I am willing.

Chapter 1

The Beginning

"Because what may be known of God is
manifest in them, for God has shown it to them.
For since the creation of the world His invisible
attributes are clearly seen, being understood
by the things that are made, even His eternal
power and Godhead, so that they are without
excuse."

Romans 1:19-20 NKVJ

My testimony begins with God's calling on my
life. In January of 1980, my mom found herself
in the hospital. She was around five months
pregnant with me and she was so sick that she
couldn't keep food down. As she recalled it to
me, I'd stopped growing in her womb. Test after
test revealed nothing. Doctors couldn't figure
out what was wrong. It would be a complicated
pregnancy for my mom. From the beginning,
the enemy wanted me dead.

In January of 2019, God gave me a vision of a demonic attack I'd experienced when I was in my mom's womb. I was born into a cursed family by way of generational traditions. The spiritual cords from the generational curses on my life were wrapped around me so tightly that my natural fetal body stopped growing. A friend later spoke the following words of knowledge to me, confirming my vision. "Someone laid spiritual hands on you while you were in the womb, claiming you for the Kingdom of God." This "spiritual laying of hands" loosened the cords on my life just enough for me to continue on til birth. My dad told me a woman went to pray over my mom when she was in the hospital with me. I believe that woman was my maternal great-grandmother.

Speaking to my mom, I would later find out that this had been the second attempt on my life. The first attempt came directly at my mom before she even knew she was pregnant with me. A man broke into the house when she was home alone. Consequently, she'd experienced an intense panic attack and had gone to the doctor to get checked. It was then that she found out she was pregnant with me.

"The LORD is righteous; He has cut in pieces the cords of the wicked."

Psalms 129:4 NKJV

My childhood was riddled with abuse because I had been born to parents who themselves were victims of abuse. I suffered at the hands of an angry and sober alcoholic father who was in denial. My mother managed, as best as she could, having suffered from traumatic childhood abuses herself; anger and vengeance were her daily outpour. I was beaten, demoralized, and unprotected, but my parents loved me the best way they knew how. A Christian therapist would later diagnose my years of struggle with debilitating depression and anxiety as complex post-traumatic stress disorder or C-PTSD.

C-PTSD is defined by Wikipedia as "a psychological disorder that can develop in response to prolonged, repeated experience of interpersonal trauma in a context in which the individual has little or no chance of escape. It shares all the symptoms of post-traumatic stress disorder such as reliving the traumatic experience, avoiding certain situations, lack of trust, insomnia, inability to concentrate and physical symptoms caused by remembering certain traumas which would otherwise have no related medical cause. Additional symptoms include: inability to control or regulate feelings, dissociation (forgetting the trauma or feeling unattached to the emotions surrounding the trauma), a hyper negative self-perception, difficulty with relationships, a biased view of the abuser and a very skewed, distrusting world view" (Source: healthline.com).

I experienced all the symptoms of C-PTSD with no real understanding of why until my mid-twenties. The answers can be traced back to my childhood.

I grew up middle class in San Antonio, Texas. We did all the normal things other families did. We celebrated holidays with extended family, went on vacations, took the obligatory family photos, albeit not yearly. On the outside, we were just like any other family of four living in the suburbs.

Both my parents had very good jobs. My mom worked at Southwestern Bell Telephone Company, which has since been acquired by AT&T. She got that job when she was 18 and stayed there until she retired in her early forties. I remember "Ma Bell", as she affectionately referred to the company, being such a huge part of our lives. My mom was part of the Communications Workers of America union. I went to work with her a handful of times. She even took me to picket with her once when they were fighting for higher wages. I always thought my mom had the best job. For the majority of her career, she was a dispatcher in the coin department. As I understand it, she dispatched repairmen and women to fix payphones all over Texas. My mom could recall locations of zip codes and area codes the way most people can recall the alphabet. She had a phenomenal photographic memory, and she excelled at her job because of it.

Before my parents met, my dad served four years in the Army. After he came home from serving overseas, he took odd jobs as a painter. When I was still very young, my dad worked for the public transportation system in San Antonio called VIA. He cleaned the busses and would bring home random treasures from time to time. I distinctly remember umbrellas. For whatever reason, people would leave their covering behind when the threat of rain disappeared. Eventually, he would hunker down and apply for an apprenticeship in electronics as civil service for the Air Force. I remember him studying while my brother and I played quietly. My dad would stay at his job with the government until he retired in his sixties.

Our family was picture perfect, but I felt like we were always keeping secrets and were not able to freely talk about home life. Talking about the dog or mentioning the parrot my dad brought home from Mexico were safe topics.

Anything that happened behind closed doors was off limits.

My parents were unknowingly abusive and our home was religious, but non-Christian. Both my parents were verbally and physically abusive to me. My older brother would suffer my dad's wrath, but in contrast, my mom met my brother with nothing but adoration. My mom's relationship with her own mother was broken and therefore, severely affected our mother/daughter relationship. Manipulation was the only love language spoken. Giving and receiving love was completely conditional and the terms expired often.

I have very clear memories of being sexually victimized by being exposed to pornography and masturbation as early as three-years old. I would struggle with addiction to both pornography and masturbation for years into my adulthood. I recall a therapist once told me that masturbating at five-years old was normal. She said children discover themselves "accidentally". This is a generally accepted point of view for secularists. A quick Google search asking, "Is it normal for children to masturbate" will return 1,450,000 results validating the normalcy of the topic. The advice ranges from when the right time to talk about it is to why masturbation for a child is considered a self-soothing technique. I can personally testify that I don't remember accidentally discovering myself. I remember seeing people masturbate in front of me in the form of pornographic media, and I learned the behavior. It would be 33 years before I was delivered from this.

As a family, we watched horror films on a regular basis. My eye gates and ear gates were completely unguarded, unprotected and abused. My parents did not know or understand the importance of praying over my eyes and ears. They didn't know why filtering what we watched and heard was important to our spiritual health. They also didn't understand God could completely redeem these important spiritual gates to the glory of His Kingdom.

"The lamp of the body is the eye. If therefore your eye is good, your whole body will be full of light. But if your eye is bad, your whole body will be full of darkness. If therefore the light that is in you is darkness, how great is that darkness!"

Matthew 6:22-23 NKJV

"My son, give attention to my words; incline your ear to my sayings. Do not let them depart from your eyes; keep them in the midst of your heart; for they are life to those who find them, and health to all their flesh."

Proverbs 4:20-22

"The hearing ear and the seeing eye, the Lord has made them both."

Proverbs 20:12 NKJV

We attended Catholic church regularly enough for my brother and I to have our first communions. After that, we were Cheaster (Christmas and Easter) attendees. I eventually tried to get my confirmation, which is the final one of the three sacraments of initiation into the Catholic Church. During the confirmation classes, I asked a lot of questions about why we were doing the things we were doing. I wanted to see specifically in the Bible where these things were mentioned. The teacher could not answer my questions, and I was forthwith labeled as disruptive. Before I could complete this sacrament, the head priest of the church scheduled a meeting with my mom and I was asked to not return to the classes or the church. I was 17.

We celebrated all the major holidays and each one was fueled with drama, usually because my mom would have an emotional outburst of sorts. My dad, on the other hand, internalized as much of his rage as he could and would wait to release it when we got home. Family camping and fishing trips were regularly dotted with violent outbursts; this would cause the trip to end prematurely. I remember one particular trip where my dad decided to self-medicate his anger by drinking beer while driving home. I was maybe eight-years old. I put up such a fuss at the risk of my physical safety to get him to stop drinking. My rationale was I would either get clobbered by my dad or we would die in a car wreck. Given my druthers, I convinced my dad to throw the beer out of the window.

Eventually, I would carry the torch for both my parents. I would become completely enraged for no reason. At one point, I was diagnosed with Bipolar disorder. Bipolar disorder does not run in my family, but psychotic illnesses like schizophrenia do. It was not hard for anyone to believe that I genuinely suffered from Bipolar disorder.

Oxford English Dictionary says that Bipolar disorder is "a mental condition marked by alternating periods of elation and depression." I was definitely symptomatic of Bipolar depression, but the diagnosis was wrong. Symptoms of Bipolar disorder, according to the Mayo Clinic, can cause unpredictable changes in mood and behavior, resulting in significant distress and difficulty in life. It is usually diagnosed in a person's teenage years or early twenties. I was in my late twenties and the therapist who misdiagnosed me did so after one interview. She sent me to a psychiatrist who would then prescribe five different antipsychotic medications to be taken simultaneously with two different anti-anxiety medications. Needless to say, the medications did not work.

On the inside, I knew my behavior was irrational, but on the outside, I had zero control over the emotions I felt. As an adult, I didn't know how to process the tsunamic waves of hurt, anger, shame, guilt, and embarrassment. As a child, I turned to self-medicating to keep myself from blowing my cover.

I started smoking when I was ten-years old and I was drinking by 12. I started using drugs (marijuana and cocaine) by 13. I was an alcoholic by the time I was 15. I also started having regular sex by this age. My rebellion was rampant.

"Rebellion is as the sin of witchcraft, and stubbornness is as iniquity and idolatry."

1 Samuel 15:23 NKJV

Despite these hardships, I was a model student. In my adolescence, I was an angry but smart girl. I challenged authority, but I was also an outstanding student. I made straight A's until high school when I earned my first C in a college level Physics class I took my sophomore year. I was an overachieving people-pleaser and I excelled on paper for this reason.

My first supernatural experience happened when I was three-years old. I encountered an angel who would be with me for the next 35 years. When I was between five and six, I encountered several other angels, and then I wouldn't have another supernatural experience until I was 15. This encounter took place when I played with a Ouija board with some neighborhood friends.

The origins of the Ouija board were a bit convoluted until recently when Ouija historian Robert Murch started his own research in

1992. It was then that he realized there wasn't much on the topic. This struck him as odd given the popularity of the board game. He discovered the earliest mention of the talking board, as it was sometimes called, in an Associated Press article from 1886. The article said "the phenomenon was sweeping Ohio" (Source: baltimoremagazine.com, *Not Dead Yet*). A little less than forty years prior, in 1848, what's known as spiritualism blew up in "America due to the popularity of the Fox sisters. They were three sisters who made a name for themselves as mediums who communicated with the dead. Articles on the sisters and other spiritualists heightened the interest in seances. This growing interest in spiritualism, coupled with a new tool to cut out the middle man, piqued the attention of an entrepreneur named Charles Kennard. In 1890, he partnered with four other investors, and together, they founded the Kennard Novelty Company. They began mass producing the Ouija boards and selling them as quickly as they were coming off the line. It would soon become the only patented game board to outsell Monopoly.

Prior to selling the boards, one of the investors named Elijah Bond, an attorney, together with his sister-in-law, a practiced medium, took the board to acquire a patent. The chief patent officer would not issue a patent for the board until it was demonstrated the board worked as they said it did. He asked for the board to spell out his name, which was said to be unknown to Bond and his sister-in-law. As the three of them sat down to play, the board correctly spelled out the name of the patent officer. He would then issue the patent for the game, albeit shaken from the experience" (Source: Smithsonianmag.com, *The Strange and Mysterious History of the Ouija Board*).

The talking board was promoted as "patented to work as advertised," which became a major selling point. It was generally accepted into society as a harmless family game that allowed family members to communicate with the other side. It wasn't until 1973 when the movie *The Exorcist,* based on a true story and adapted from a book, portrayed the game as a gateway to the demonic realm.

"The Exorcist, the book, was written in 1971. The author, William Peter Blatty, said his original intent of writing the novel was to "scare a generation into going back to church." Blatty based his book on real life events surrounding a young boy several newspapers referred to as 'Robbie' or 'Roland Doe'. The newspapers reported an apparent possession and exorcism of Robbie, who lived in Cottage City, Maryland at the time, in 1949. Blatty is said to have heard about the story during his enrollment at Georgetown University. He took details from Robbie's reported experiences as well as details from a series of exorcisms known as the Loudun exorcisms of 1634 to write the supernaturally based horror book" (Source: atgtickets.com, *The real life exorcism that inspired The Exorcist...*).

"The movie was then based on the events of the book. The movie depicted in detail a young girl's possession of a demonic spirit after playing with a Ouija board. The movie received mixed reviews, but this did not stop people from going in masses to see the horror flick. The film was said to inflict its viewers with adverse experiences such as miscarriages and heart attacks" (Source: Klemesrud, Judy (January 27, 1974). "They Wait Hours to Be Shocked". *The New York Times.* Archived from the original on March 1, 2019. Retrieved March 1, 2019).

"In 1975, a psychiatric paper was published documenting four different cases of 'cinematic neurosis' or trauma due to watching the film (Source: Bozzuto, James C. (July 1, 1975). "Cinematic neurosis following "The Exorcist": Report of four cases". *The Journal of Nervous and Mental Disease*). Film historian William Paul speculated no other film has ever had quite the effect on the audience as has *The Exorcist"*.

Prior to the production of the movie and subsequent zeal on the topic of Ouija boards and possession, the author began using a board himself. He referred to it as research for his book. During this time, Blatty was convinced demonic possession was real and had his own supernatural experiences. He is quoted saying:

> "For the first time in my life, I got hung up on a Ouija board for ten days. I'd never done it before but I found I couldn't leave it alone. And I had the most definite feeling that I was communicating with the dead."

After Blatty's experimentation with the board, he continued to have unexplainable experiences:

> "But then there were poltergeist experiences. Revising the book at a friend's house, the telephone rang and suddenly the receiver leapt off the hook. It happened to him first and then to me. So I asked a friend who did the acoustics for the Kennedy Center what the possibilities were electrically and he said it was impossible. Then telephone engineers in two states confirmed that it was impossible. But we both saw it

happen. That was the culmination of several incidents, but it was the one that in no way could be explained."

"An electric typewriter wrote a line of gibberish, but what do I know about electricity. Maybe there was a short circuit somewhere. That was possible." (Source: Aleteia.com, Caldwell, Zelda, *What happened when the author of 'The Exorcist' played with a Ouija board*, published 10/30/17).

The Ouija board is a flat board marked with the alphabet listed in a half circle above the numbers zero through nine in another half circle. "Yes" and "No" are in the two upper corners and "goodbye" is at the bottom of the board. Depending on where you get one, the boards can be more intricately decorated with various other designs and symbols, while others are plain with just letters, numbers and words. The boards come with a tool called a planchette, which is used to "point" to the various board markings, be it the letters, numbers, words or symbols. The board will work properly when two or more people come into agreement to play the game.

The Ouija board I played with was one sold by Hasbro. Hasbro acquired Parker Brothers who bought the rights to the game from the last living investor of the original four. My neighbors had the board in their garage, and one day while I was over at their house, they asked if I wanted to play with the board. I had seen *The Exorcist* many times and there was an inner fear that told me I shouldn't, but I succumbed to peer pressure, believing that it would be harmless. I remember sitting on the floor in the garage with the two other girls. I was nervous about playing the game, but I didn't think anything would happen. I don't remember the first question we asked, but I do remember the lights in the garage started to flicker and a loud bang came from the garage door as if something hit it very hard. I remember sensing a lot of anger, but I didn't understand why. It was at this point that we got scared and put the game away.

About two weeks later, I remember going to my dad in tears. I had been having nightmares and I thought it had to do with me playing with the Ouija board. When I told my dad what I had done, he responded, "Well, whatever happens to you now from playing that game is going to be punishment enough." I was dismissed in tears. One of my neighbors would say her older brother banged the garage door from the outside, but that still didn't explain the lights flickering or the intense anger I sensed.

It was at this point that rebellion and depression took over. When suicide failed me, I started burning and cutting myself. I have since been healed of these physical and emotional scars, save for one faded burn on my leg. After this, I encountered demonic angels often. I struggled with containing anger, on top of dealing with depression and anxiety, both in which I didn't understand. Sometimes, the putrid smell of rotten eggs would engulf my room. It wouldn't be until later that I would understand why.

When I was 17, I got into a fistfight with my dad. It was one of the more severe clashes we had. It was also the first time I didn't back down. My mom tried to break up the fight, and when she got between us, I accidentally hit her. This enraged my father even more. He palmed the side of my head and bashed it into the wall. I saw the blackness of a knockout briefly as I recovered from the pain ringing through my head. I recall my mom yelling at my dad to stop before he did it again. I wasn't entirely lucid, but I was alert enough to know I needed to leave. I was angry and confused.

I went to my then boyfriend's house and told his mom what happened. I'll never forget. She quoted Ephesians 6:12 and explained that our fight wasn't against flesh and blood. Then she quoted Exodus 20:12 and explained how I had behaved wrongly. She was speaking directly to my spirit, but my flesh wouldn't listen. I couldn't understand. How was I wrong? My dad beat me. I was defending myself. How was I supposed to honor that?! She grabbed my hands and started praying for me. It was the first time I ever heard anyone pray in tongues over me, fighting for my spiritual life. I pulled away from her, but she was relentless. She didn't let go of my hands and continued praying in the Spirit. I was frightened but mesmerized at the same time.

"Likewise the Spirit also helps in our weaknesses. For we do not know what we should pray for as we ought, but the Spirit Himself makes intercession for us with groanings which cannot be uttered. Now He who searches the hearts knows what the mind of the Spirit is, because He makes intercession for the saints according to the will of God."

Romans 8:26-27 NKJV

Chapter 2

Meeting God

A month after I turned 18, I left my parent's house to escape the manipulative and controlling abuse. It was also during this time that I started going to a Spirit-filled, Bible-based church. They operated highly in the supernatural movement and anointing of Holy Spirit. The first time someone laid hands on me, before I was even saved, I was slain in the Spirit, meaning I was overcome by the power of Holy Spirit. Sometimes, people will fall to the floor or lose their ability to balance themselves when the weight of the power of God is upon them. I fell to the floor.

After I got saved, I experienced the intense joy of the Spirit many, many times. I had no clue what was happening to me, but I remember going home, opening my new student Bible and finding 1 Peter 1:8-9 in the NIV translation, which reads, "Though you have not seen him, you love him; and even though you do not see him now, you believe in him and are filled with an inexpressible and glorious joy, for you are receiving the goal of your faith, the salvation of your souls." I was so blown away by what happened that I called my drug dealer and witnessed to him.

Despite my newfound faith, I continued to live a life of promiscuity until I got pregnant at the age of 22. Although I was saved and knew Christ, and didn't live at home anymore, I had an abortion at the demand of my father, who was under the influence of a controlling, manipulative spirit. This experience was a red flag indicator of a negative soul tie or yoke I had with my dad, but I had no reason to know what that was or that it even existed. I would eventually break the ties of this yoke after twenty more years.

"He is a double-minded man, unstable in all he does."

James 1:8 NIV

By 25, I was water baptized and received the baptism of the Holy Spirit. It was during this time I experienced my first deliverance. When I received Holy Spirit, I started throwing up violently. My spiritual mom at the time told me Holy Spirit was getting the "junk out of me." God delivered me from alcoholism and drugs. I was so on fire for God that I didn't think anything would deter me. I was naïve to think this first deliverance would be my last. No one went into depth about the cleansing of my soul. I was accountable to church leadership, but this would not suffice in maintaining my deliverance.

I managed to graduate college with two Associate degrees and a Bachelor of Business Administration in Computer Information Systems. I landed a solid job, lived in a nice apartment, owned a lovely car and bought my first motorcycle. I stopped drinking and partying; everything seemed perfect.

When I was 27, I met a Christian man who would later become my husband. We were married in 2008, planted in a Spirit-filled, Bible-based church, serving, tithing and attending a small group. We were connected. Rebellion was gone and I was on the road to a new life. He was deployed for a year, came home, and in 2011, wanted a divorce. He told me this by text while he was on assignment in another state.

The divorce broke me. The very core of who I was shattered instantaneously. People at church shunned me. I attempted suicide again.

Looking back, I believe God sent an angel of intervention because the gun would not fire. Unbeknownst to me, the gun jammed. I wouldn't find this out until months later when a police officer came to my house as a courtesy to inspect the home's safety, including firearms. He inspected all the guns and asked how that particular one got jammed. I had no clue.

During the divorce, I relapsed into drugs and an immoral lifestyle. I turned against God and eventually found myself swallowed up by the world. For the next six years, God would be knocking on my door and I refused to answer. It would be in the seventh year that I could not ignore Him any longer, but more on that later.

I left the house I had purchased with my ex-husband and moved into a tiny studio apartment with my cat, Zoe, and my dog, Dozer. These two were my only companions for the next few months until I met Art.

Dozer was a full-grown Bullmastiff. At his heaviest, he weighed 180 pounds. He was the gentlest giant around, albeit clumsy. He constantly stepped on my feet, got in the path of my legs, and basically ran me over in his awkward excitement. One day, I was taking Dozer for his afternoon walk. As he was copping a squat to do his business, I noticed a man riding a beautiful, shiny white M109 cruiser motorcycle.

The more I stared, the more I felt infatuated with his Gucci good looks. He was in excellent physical shape, clean-cut and his bike was stunning. Before I could turn away, he rode past me, smiled and waved at me. I stumbled over Dozer while he was still squatting and fell on the ground. I was so embarrassed. I suppose it made a memorable impression. A few days later, Art introduced himself to me properly. We became friends and mostly hung out going on motorcycle rides together.

Art quickly became a staple in my life, and it didn't take long for him to see the real me. From the outside, it looked like I had my life together. However, adjusting your life from a two-income household to a one-income household can be challenging, especially when you are a drug addict being swallowed alive by depression and anxiety. Art's friendship kept me from drowning. We were mutually interested in one another, so we soon started dating.

After moving from San Antonio to Dallas to further isolate myself from my family, I married Art in 2013 and we had our first daughter in 2014. This was followed by two years of the worst depression I had experienced thus far. My doctor would diagnose me with Postpartum Depression or PPD.

Oxford Languages says "PPD is depression suffered by a mother following childbirth, typically arising from the combination of hormonal changes, psychological adjustment to motherhood, and fatigue. This mood disorder is said to affect both the mother and father. Symptoms include sadness, lack of energy, anxiety, off and on crying, insomnia or oversleeping and changes in appetite."

What I had felt worse than PPD. I had already experienced depression and anxiety, so I was familiar with having all of those symptoms, but this was a whole new experience. I felt like I leveled up in a whole new way to sadness and out of control anxiety. I battled for hours, convincing myself to leave the house to check the mail. I would freak out when someone other than my husband called me, which thankfully, didn't happen often. I would pace back and forth through the duplex we lived in, checking the windows and back door for anything that might be lurking outside. Thinking back, I do not know why I was so fearful, but I now know it was spiritual.

The most damaging thing that happened to me was losing my identity in Christ. I forgot what God had already brought me out of. I forgot I had already been delivered once before. No one taught me how to maintain this deliverance, and I didn't search it out for myself. I honestly didn't realize I needed to maintain it.

In Dallas, I didn't have family or friends, other than my husband. I also became embattled with my parents over the birth of my daughter. I ended up cutting my entire family out of my life for two years. I was severely depressed, isolated, back on drugs and anxiety ruled my life.

"When an evil spirit comes out of a man, it goes through arid places seeking rest and does not find it. Then it says, 'I will return to the house I left.' When it arrives, it finds the house unoccupied, swept clean and put in order. Then it goes and takes with it seven other spirits more wicked than itself, and they go in and live there. And the final condition of that man is worse than the first. That is how it will be with this wicked generation."

Matthew 12:43-45 NIV

"The secret things belong to the Lord our God, but those things which are revealed belong to us and to our children forever, that we may do all the words of this law."

Deuteronomy 29:29 NKJV

In late 2016, right before our daughter turned two, our garage in Dallas was broken into, and we were completely cleaned out. We were living in an apartment above the garage in a very urban area. It was a concrete jungle amidst bars and restaurants on the popular Knox/Henderson strip. Walking out the front door of the apartment onto the deck provided a view overlooking a dumpster and the parking lot to three bars. The backside was an alley to apartment complexes, and next door to the right were sorority houses. The left side was lined with bars. Hearing people come and go from their vehicles all weekend was a norm. Like clockwork, we would hear the stumbles of people finding their way home via the alley at two in the morning when the bars would close. When we heard people yelling downstairs, there was no reason to be alarmed.

My husband and I had been watching a movie while our daughter slept. As per usual, I was already high and not entirely coherent. When the movie ended, we got ourselves ready for bed, brushed our teeth and settled down for the night. When I walked into our bedroom from the restroom, I heard a man's voice, "Hurry, we gotta go!" After that, I heard two doors slam and a vehicle drive off. I tucked myself into bed and fell asleep.

The next morning as we were leaving to work, I noticed one of the doors to the garage was slightly open. When I walked inside, almost everything we owned had been stolen. We had brand new camping equipment and tools, baby furniture, my husband's mementos from his deployments – all gone. All our motorcycle gear was taken as well. The feelings of loss and violation prompted my husband and me to move back to San Antonio and eventually buy a house in New Braunfels.

Looking back, I can see how God was all over this move. The insurance money we received after the theft helped us secure a house. The house we bought was originally way out of our price range, but overnight, the price dropped by over $20,000 and we were able to buy it. God was gently guiding me, even though I didn't know it.

Before we moved from Dallas, I had quit my high-stress job in property management and started exercising daily. I walked the neighborhood we lived in and I happened upon a community garden. The lady who was tending to the growing produce happened to be the lady in charge. I stopped to talk with her and left with a new commitment of volunteering twice a week. It was exciting because I got to spend time doing something I really enjoyed and I was allowed take any extra vegetables they might have. This new opportunity prompted me to start eating better and taking better care of my physical body. This was the first step I took in my journey to kick drug addiction.

By early 2017, I'd fallen so far into depression that I sought the guidance of another therapist, but specifically, a secular therapist. The last therapist I had seen four years prior was a Spirit-filled Christian. He told me to get off drugs and get connected to a church. I got clean for six months and relapsed. I quit drugs again during the pregnancy of my first daughter and relapsed again after I stopped nursing her. I never found a church. This new, non-Christian therapist offered me the hope I wanted. Zero accountability to Christ and everything the world had to offer. I was absolutely determined to get clean and healthy. I was desperate for it. I did not want my daughter to grow up with a drug addicted mother who had depression and anxiety. Therapy seemed like a great next step.

During my first session, I remember very specifically telling the therapist I knew God was coming after me and I didn't want to have anything to do with Him. I also told the therapist something was wrong with me. There was no reason for me to be as depressed as I was. I was working out daily, eating very clean, my child was a great kid, my husband was amazing... we had it all. The house, the vehicles, the dogs – I had plenty of reasons to be enjoying life, but I couldn't. I was angry and miserable, despite having all the right material things.

Over the course of several months, I was encouraged to explore my passions, but never discouraged to quit drugs.

Chapter 3

The Craft

The more I explored, the more I was drawn to the occult. It was subtle at first. It started with my love for plants, which turned to herbalism, and then green magic.

After six months of research, I was full blown sucked into the world of witchcraft. I self-identified as a green witch and belonged to an online coven. A green witch is a person who uses plants, stones and essential oils as their main tools of the craft. Incantations and spells are used in conjunction with plants and herbs. Specific plants are said to have specific mystical qualities and can be used to bring good luck, provide protection, ward off evil spirits, and so forth.

A green witch will use all things in nature to bring forth herbal and energy healing. A person practicing green magic might also use stones and gems to help foster communication with the land, animals and other people. Green magic appears to be very harmless. Some green witches will identify themselves as very spiritual and believing in a higher power or being. Some green witches worship mother earth, and there are even some who would self-identify as Christian. This is called mixture. I will touch more on this in the following pages.

A coven is a group of witches who practice their craft together. They fellowship together and establish a sense community with each other. There is a strong acceptance within their social sects. Although somewhat secretive, they were definitely unified. Some believed this would make their magic stronger. Most witches I knew belonged to a group. I was still "in the broom closet", which meant that I didn't publicly announce my affiliation with the occult. Belonging to an online coven allowed for some anonymity with the perks of gaining knowledge. Not surprisingly, a lot of the witches I knew who were still in the broom closet had a Christian background.

I followed the rule of "do no harm," meaning none of the magic I performed was intended to cause any other person, animal or living thing (plants) harm unless I wanted it to come back to me threefold. Some witches and warlocks did not follow this rule because they either didn't believe in it or believed their magic was strong enough to counteract any backlash. Others believed as I did; if you intended to harm another person with your craft, you opened the door to bringing that fate onto yourself or your family. It is a spiritual rule that is actually biblical.

"Therefore, whatever you want men to do to you, do also to them, for this is the Law and the Prophets."
                                        Matthew 7:12 NKJV

As I was exploring all things occult, I began reconciling my relationship with God. I reasoned that He wanted me to be happy and I was finally finding some kind of happiness. For these reasons, I believed I was a Christian witch. There is no such thing as a Christian witch, but I believed it nonetheless. It intrigued me to find out that many witches use Bible scriptures in their incantations. This is another reason why some people might believe that practicing a craft is acceptable. They might think using Bible scriptures make their crafts "Christian", but all it is doing is invalidating the power and authority they would walk in if they relied on Jesus. This is mixture and is absolutely witchcraft.

I'd forgotten everything I learned in church about the occult. It never dawned on me the road I was on was one of deceit. The spirit of seduction had come upon me to draw me further into rebellion more than I realized.

"Rather, that the things which the Gentiles sacrifice they sacrifice to demons and not to God, and I do not want you to have fellowship with demons. You cannot drink the cup of the Lord and the cup of demons; you cannot partake of the Lord's table and of the table of demons."

I Corinthians 10:20-21 NKJV

At the encouragement of my secular therapist, I started practicing sigil magic, which is a form of written magic. I was also reading palms, slinging (tarot) cards as it is called, casting spells, and smudging.

"For example, never sacrifice your son or daughter as a burnt offering. And do not let your people practice fortune-telling, or use sorcery, or interpret omens, or engage in witchcraft, or cast spells, or function as mediums or psychics, or call forth the spirits of the dead."

Deuteronomy 18:10-11 NLT

Smudging happens to be an extremely popular practice. It is also called "saging" because one burns the herb sage with the belief that it will help in spiritually cleansing their home. Doing this actually opens the door to demonic activity. It allows for demonic possession of the dwelling in which it is performed because it is witchcraft.

Some will argue that this only happens when the practice is done wrong; that it has to be done in conjunction with Palo Santo, a medicinal tree native to most South American countries. The belief is that sage opens the door in the spirit realm, allowing the evil spirits to leave, and burning Palo Santo closes the door. This isn't true. Whether you do the practice with or without Palo Santo, it is harmful witchcraft.

In addition to smudging, I was also doing self-hypnosis under the influence of drugs. I also dabbled in energy work known as Reiki healing. I learned about chakras, energy blockages and restoring flow to these blocked areas. I would eventually set up a prayer altar in my closet complete with incantations, oils, incense and my journal. This perfect combination of occult practices left me intoxicated and wide open to demonization.

"Be sober, be vigilant; because your adversary the devil walks about like a roaring lion, seeking whom he may devour."

1 Peter 5:8 NKJV

Of all the different forms of witchcraft, I was specifically and strongly drawn to sigil magic. A sigil is an inscribed or painted symbol considered to have magical power. It is magic written out in the form of symbols which have been created through a process of intentional manipulation. The focus is to create a symbol which embodies a personal desire and cause it to manifest. These symbols can represent a manifested deity, which is said to have never existed until the symbol was created.

The truth is, a demon waits for a person to give focused and intentional energy to a made-up symbol, which in turn gives the demon legal rights to manifest in the person's life. It is a perversion of the scribe anointing. It takes the power and authority of a person anointed by Holy Spirit to write and it twists their gift for the benefit of the kingdom of darkness.

Symbolism is very prevalent in the occult. Everything means something because it is meant to draw your attention away from the real meaning. Take the rainbow for instance. God created the rainbow as a reminder of His promise that He would not flood the Earth again:

"I do set my bow in the cloud, and it shall be for a token of a covenant between me and the earth. And it shall come to pass, when I bring a cloud over the earth, that the bow shall be seen in the cloud: And I will remember my covenant, which is between me and you and every living creature of all flesh; and the waters shall no more become a flood to destroy all flesh. And the bow shall be in the cloud; and I will look upon it, that I may remember the everlasting covenant between God and every living creature of all flesh that is upon the earth. And God said unto Noah, This is the token of the covenant, which I have established between me and all flesh that is upon the earth."

Genesis 9:13-17 KJV

In current times, the rainbow has become a

symbol of the lesbian, gay, bisexual, transgender and queer movement. It is a way for the devil to instill a lie very subtly. If you don't know the origin of a thing, it becomes very easy to fall into the trap of symbolism. This is a very commonly used tactic of the enemy. He will provide a lie to replace the unknown truth.

During this season of practicing witchcraft, I honestly did not know what the scribe anointing was, much less that I might possibly have this anointing. One of the reasons I was drawn to sigil magic is because I am gifted in writing. It comes very naturally to me. The first time I realized this, I was in high school in an advanced placement English class. I had written a paper overnight and received a 99. One point was deducted because I overlooked a period on the bibliography page.

Other indicators of my gift for writing surfaced in junior college. I was talking to a college counselor about transfer credits for university when she looked at my transcripts and said,

"Well, before we do that, we need to put your applications in for your Associate degrees." I responded "I already did. I received my Associate of Applied Science in the mail." To which, she said, "April, you have enough credits here for an Associate of Arts degree. Why haven't you already applied for it?" I didn't know I could. I took those classes because they were easy for me. It is no different from a person who takes multiple physical education classes because they are athletic and enjoy the activities.

Through most of college, I researched and wrote papers easily. I even earned side income while writing papers for the upper classmen, guaranteeing them a B or better. If they wanted a C, and sometimes this was the case, it was a much harder paper for me to write. I thought most people could write well and the people who hired me were simply too busy to write.

Going back to sigil magic—the enemy knew I was gifted in writing, so he worked hard to pervert and steal this gift, even from my adolescence. When I was 15, my mom read my journal. How she and my dad handled the contents of my journal severely damaged my trust in writing. I didn't start writing again for over twenty years. The enemy will always try to snuff out your God-given gifts, which are the greatest threats to his kingdom of darkness.

Take King David, for example. You'll notice that as a young man, he was a sheepherder or shepherd. Oftentimes, people focus on the fact that David learned his skills as a rock slinger by protecting the sheep. One thing that goes unnoticed is that in order for David to have harnessed the power for the rock sling, he had to first have keen eyesight. His vision had to be sharp to spot any predators sneaking in for the kill. His vision also had to be sharp for the day he would kill Goliath. He would spot his target, and in one swift motion, the giant would go down. King David's eyes were a gift. He had keen sight. Many years later, his eyes caught the sight of Bathsheba while she was bathing. This perverted his eye gates and led to one of the most historic downfalls of King David's life.

Chapter 4

Familiar Spirits and Generational Curses

Witchcraft feels very intuitive to the practitioner. One reason is because the enemy manipulates your God-given gifts. Another reason is because of familiar spirits and generational curses.

"The LORD is longsuffering, and of great mercy, forgiving iniquity and transgression, and by no means clearing the guilty, visiting the iniquity of the fathers upon the children unto the third and fourth generation."

Numbers 14:18 KJV

I was familiar with witchcraft because my paternal grandmother openly practiced witchcraft, but called it traditional medicine. Whenever I was sick and my grandmother was around, she would bring out an egg. Hispanic and specifically Mexican culture fears "el ojo" or what is also known as the evil eye. During a series of prayers that are really incantations, the egg is rubbed over the body and it is said to absorb whatever it is that has been afflicting the body. The egg is then cracked and placed into water. People who do this believe that if the egg floats, you're cured of whatever affliction you had. If it sinks, you're cursed.

The reliance on the egg, the ritual and the subsequent incantation to bring about healing, rather than trusting in God, Son, Holy Spirit and the Word, makes this full-blown witchcraft hiding in a traditional belief system. That belief system secures the curse within the core of this practice. Doors to demonic activity are being swung wide open every time these traditions are passed to the next generation. This then becomes a generational curse.

These are not the only memories I hold of my paternal grandmother. Grandma used to spend the night at my parents' house, and she would sleep in my room with me. I remember that her sleep was very disturbed and interrupted. She was often traumatized by demonic spirits. I remember lying in bed with her and she would convulse in her sleep. It wasn't like a normal twitch. It was her full body. She would shake so badly that the bed would move.

I also remember being next to her and feeling something else in the room with us. I never saw anything, but I knew something else was with us. It got to the point that when Grandma would stay over, I was too afraid to stay in my room with her. I would wait till everyone was asleep, and then sleep on the floor in my brother's room. I was five or six when this happened.

My grandmother also suffered from schizophrenia. I was told that it manifested early in her life. When she wasn't stoned on medication, she would sit and pray for hours at a time. She wasn't always aware of her surroundings, but praying allowed for a peaceful time for her. It was an unintelligible praying. We didn't know if she was speaking

English, French or Spanish, as she was fluent in all three languages. I think she was praying the rosary. I'm not even sure she was consciously aware that she was praying.

I didn't find out until I became an adult that her father had been a curandero. A curandero can also be called a shaman, a witch doctor, a healer or a warlock, depending on the culture it is practiced in. In the Hispanic culture, a curandero is usually the paternal head of the family whom people seek out for herbal medicines and healing incantations. When I had revelation of this information, I realized I was the fourth generation in the bloodline to receive this curse. Not surprisingly, three cousins on my dad's side of the family are witches. I haven't talked to them in over twenty years and I didn't know this until I looked them up on social media at the prompting of Holy Spirit.

Sometimes, generational curses are difficult to identify. You don't ask, no one talks about it and everyone ignores the proverbial elephant in the room. When you grow up in a dysfunctional family or environment, you simply don't know the elephant in the room isn't supposed to be there. For example, I was experiencing the supernatural as a young child, but it wasn't until the darkness came that I started being told why I was experiencing it. The demons started lies about why I was the way I was, and it was easy to believe because the truth hadn't yet been revealed to me.

However, God will strategically place people in your life to reveal and uncover those demonic things. I remember in high school, after telling a close friend about one of my mom's normal breakdowns, my friend said to me, "April, that's not normal." Again, in college, a good friend told me, "April, something is wrong; you shouldn't be so angry." In my mid-twenties, a coworker named Gene told me that it wasn't normal for five-year old kids to watch horror films.

It was particularly interesting how that conversation came about. I was explaining to

Gene how my fiancé had never seen any of the classic supernatural horror films: The Exorcist, The Omen, The Amityville Horror, and so forth. I asked her if she had seen them, and she said no. "Wow, really? I grew up watching those movies!" I replied incredulously. "April, I would never show my kids or my grandkids those movies. That's not right." I felt a little foolish.

Years later, I would discuss these things with my father after our broken relationship had been completely restored. Even at sixty-eight years old, being one of the smartest men I've ever known, my dad didn't know that our family's behavior wasn't normal. He would often ask me about my husband's family, in particular, his parents. "Well, what about Art's dad? How is he?" Or he would inquire, "Did his mom ever — fill in the dysfunctional blank—?" "No Dad," I would explain, "Art's parents aren't like that. His dad is kind and sweet. His mom made a very pointed effort not to be negative."

And then, I would recall to my dad how when my oldest daughter was months old, a karate movie came on tv and my father-in-law immediately changed the channel, telling us it was too violent for her little eyes. I would also tell him how in my own miscalculation, I always thought my mother-in-law was living in denial because she literally only saw the bright side of things. Even when I was assaulted by their next-door neighbor and came home to my mother-in-law in a panic and tears, her first reaction was to gently ask me if maybe I misinterpreted the man's actions. She wasn't in denial, she always erred on the side of people having the benefit of doubt. None of this was normal for my family. I was raised on popcorn and horror movies. Accusations were like compliments. Violent eruptions of nonsense were normal in my family. We didn't know differently.

All these things that came to fruition in my life were already there due to the generational curses, however, they just took time to manifest. There was addiction, abuse, anger, offense, witchcraft, pornography, rebellion, and mental illnesses such as schizophrenia on my dad's side. My mom's side carried witchcraft, abortion, divorce, depression, anxiety and incest.

I was seduced into the occult by a familiar spirit of rebellion and generational curses. Abuse, addiction, divorce, abortion, isolation, deceit, rejection, unforgiveness… all opened doors to the demonic, and then I started occult practices. I did everything the Bible warns against, short of blood sacrifice. Just to be clear, anything not of God is of the enemy. To say this more plainly, if you're not worshiping God, you're in bondage to Satan.

God is not a seducer. He does not have to seduce us into believing Him because He is self-testifying. The enemy, on the other hand, will do everything in his given power to seduce you into believing his lies.

Chapter 5

Demonized

I remember very vividly the days the demons gained access to my internal self, no longer oppressing me from the outside. It happened over several instances, of which I will recount two. I had been a self-proclaimed witch for about four months. I was doing drugs daily and practicing guided self-hypnosis almost every night.

The first time I remember giving access to the demonic spirits was while I was in the shower. I was high after smoking a significant amount of marijuana. While I was in the shower, I started connecting to my spirit guides, which were really just demonic spirits. Connecting to them meant I was consciously communicating with them by listening to them and talking out loud back to them. They can't read your mind, but they do like to talk a lot.

I was having conversations with a familiar spirit specifically about my family. This one particular demon was telling me about my mom. It told me that my mom didn't really have a split personality (she had been diagnosed previously), but that she was like me and had connected with her spirit guides unknowingly. What the demon meant was that my mom had been demonized to the point that she would lose time and talk as if she were a completely different person. This was a demonic manifestation.

I recall one time I went to lunch with my mom. I got high in the car before going inside the restaurant. This was normal for me. While I was talking to my mom, the demon manifested for a split second and said, "If you have any extra, you know your mom used to smoke it." It freaked me out. Just as quickly as it surfaced, it went away and my mom had no idea what had just happened. I would use this information later to help my mom be delivered.

That night, as I continued to connect with these

demons, my physical body started breaking out in welts all over my face. It looked like a mosquito had a field day on my face, except there wasn't any itching. I remember looking at myself in the mirror and wondering what had happened. While I examined my face, I had this sense that I was not the only one looking. I felt something else within me looking back at me. I honestly thought I'd smoked some bad weed and was having a physical reaction. Thinking back, this made no sense. I had smoked weed for twenty years and never had this kind of reaction before. I was also never paranoid about something looking back at me in the mirror other than myself.

The next time I experienced internal demonization was a few weeks later. I was high as per usual, but this time, I was listening to a self-hypnosis audio video while I was lying in bed. I was in that state of relaxation right before you fall asleep when I felt this sudden surge of cold energy come over my body. I believe it entered through my mouth and I felt it ripple down my neck and split down my arms, traveling through my veins. It reached the tips of my fingers and rippled back through my arms, to my chest and into my belly. I felt it swirl in my belly until the feeling went away. As the energy traveled through my body, I remember a song they sang to me. I say "they" because the song had many different voices singing in unison. They only said one word: "Hello." The way they said it was what I imagine synchronized swimming would be like if it could sing. It was the most beautiful sound I had ever heard. This should not be surprising because Satan as Lucifer was an anointed cherub (Ezekiel 28:14), and it is commonly believed that he was at the very least, musical in nature (Ezekiel 28:13). I fell asleep shortly after this infestation.

When I woke up, all the voices that had sung to me the night before were now talking nonstop. They were vying for my attention like a hungry child. The chatter was incessant. At first, it was amusing, but then it became extremely bothersome. I remember having a conversation with the voices, all of which came from the demons that were inside my body. I asked one question and they all started talking at the same time. I thought I was about to lose my mind. I yelled loudly, "SHUT UP! Only one of you speak, and if you can't decide who, then no one speaks!" There was complete silence until the dominant demon's voice identified itself as "Higher Self".

The term "higher self" has a bit of ambiguity depending on the definition you reference. Wikipedia defines it as "a term associated with multiple belief systems, but its basic premise describes an eternal, omnipotent, conscious, and intelligent being, who is one's real self." Collins English dictionary describes it as "a person's spiritual self, as the focus of many meditation techniques, as opposed to the physical body." If you do a quick search on Amazon, there are books, tarot cards, oracle cards, and yoga techniques all related to communicating with your higher self. It is a concept which transcends cultures, religions and time. This is a very common descriptor for things of the occult.

There is a huge desire within the world of witchcraft to connect with your higher self. When I shared with my online coven that I had made a connection and was hearing from my higher self regularly, my confession was met with surprise. There had been witches and warlocks in their practices for years who had not attained this level of "awareness" as it was referred to. Here I was, a baby witch, on the scene for mere months and I had regular contact with this higher self. I postulate that I experienced this type of acceleration in the craft because I was baptized in the Holy Spirit. I had a target on my spirit. If I had known my true identity, power and authority in Christ, I would have been a formidable opponent to the kingdom of darkness. At best, I was a pawn for the devil.

"And you also were included in Christ when you heard the word of truth, the gospel of your salvation. Having believed, you were marked in him with a seal, the promised Holy Spirit."

Ephesians 1:13 NIV

The Higher Self spirit was in competition with Ego, another demonic spirit I had come in contact with many times. Between the two, I noticed Ego was very self-oriented and liked to focus on a victim mentality. Higher Self, on the other hand, was very empowering, very matter of fact and it often gave me this feeling of turning my nose up at the world. Ego wanted the attention of the world, but Higher Self felt the world was beneath it. Neither of them were beneficial to my sanity.

Throughout all this, I was still in therapy. My therapist was so intrigued with what was happening to me that she gave me her personal number and asked me to text her anytime with updates as to what I was experiencing. At this time, I truly had no clue I was being demonized, but the things I was experiencing should have been a clue.

During one therapy session, I told my therapist I knew she was facing a lawsuit from her old practice. A demonic spirit relayed this information to me right before our session started. My therapist was completely flabbergasted at my knowledge of her private life. She had not shared this or anything else with me, but I began to know all kinds of things about her. I told her I knew she practiced meditation, I knew she practiced yoga and I knew she was desiring a quick resolution to the impending lawsuit. She actually started crying when the session was over, and it was at this point, she gave me her number.

On the way home from therapy, I was talking to the demons and Higher Self said, "Let's have some fun." I said, "Yeah, sure!" The demon then had me close my eyes and drive through traffic, weaving in and out between cars. It was telling me which way to go and how fast or slow to go. I am convinced I was not one hundred percent in control. This only lasted a few minutes before I snapped out of it and opened my eyes.

I was connecting with demonic spirits and hallucinating, but I was so deceived that I thought I had met my spirit guides who were giving me "visions." These demonic spirits told me I was pregnant with twins, and for the next month I would believe I was physically pregnant.

Chapter 6

Michael, the Archangel

Throughout this time, I had reconnected with my parents after having cut them out of the picture for two years. I was living in New Braunfels now, which was much closer to San Antonio than Dallas. After our relationship slowly reunited, I began sharing my occult experiences with my dad.

My dad always had a flair for the supernatural. One of his pastimes was binge watching shows about unidentified flying objects, aliens, and other unexplained phenomenon. He had books on the topics and randomly shared stories of things he had experienced himself. My dad and I finally had some common ground to walk on that wasn't full of eggshells, offense and abuse. Despite our shared interest, something had my dad on alert; I'm uncertain of what that was exactly.

I had gone to the mall with my husband. Our daughter was in school and we used the day to take our computer in for repairs. While my husband was consulting with the repair technician, something was pulling my attention to another store. I had this uneasy feeling, and when I tried to consult with Higher Self, the demon remained uncharacteristically quiet.

I walked across the mall to a store that sold beautiful Turkish lamps. They were handmade, intricately designed mosaic glass. The color combinations were so creative and original. I wanted one until I saw the price tag. When I realized the lamps were out of my budget, I started to leave the store. As I was walking away, I felt this wall of energy direct my attention to something else in the store. I recognized the energy as an angel, but it was very unique. I had never felt such a strong angelic presence. The magnified energy gently guided me to another display within the store.

The display had bookmarks and door banners decorated with the same angel. I saw a warrior sitting on a horse with a sword in one hand and a shield in the other. He was covered in golden armor, including a helmet and breastplate. Every time I tried to walk away, I felt this angelic presence insist on keeping me in the store. I finally asked the store owner what these bookmarks and banners signified. He told me they were pictures of the Archangel Michael.

I immediately saw an angel reveal itself to me. I could hear it talking, telling me my dad had asked God to send the angel as protection over me. The angel told me to heed the warning that God would continue to cover me, but I needed to turn away from sorcery. The angel left as suddenly as it appeared. I left the store to call my dad.

Michael is mentioned several times in the Bible. He is known as the leader of God's angelic army. He shows up in the book of Daniel to come against the prince of Persia. After Daniel fasts for 21 days, Michael is dispatched to help overcome the demonic entity. In Jude, Michael is referred to as the archangel. He is contending with the devil over the body of Moses. In Revelation, Michael is mentioned again fighting against the dragon alongside an army of angels. He is definitely a warring angel.

When I reached out to my dad, I told him I had an encounter with the archangel, Michael. I told my dad what happened in the store and how the angel of God both appeared and spoke to me. My dad was in shock. He said he had been worried about me and all the occult stuff I had gotten myself involved in. He told me that he wasn't sure if God heard him, but he'd specifically asked God to send the archangel Michael to protect me.

A few weeks later, I was at the movies with my husband. As we were intently watching the movie, I heard a very loud and audible voice ask, "What are you doing? Do you really believe all this? Do you really believe all this is real?" I recognized the voice as the archangel Michael whom I'd previously met once before.

It startled me to the point that I sat up in my chair and looked around the theater to see if anyone else heard the voice. The voice seemed to drown out the movie itself; I heard it so clearly. When I realized I was the only one who had heard this voice, I started wondering.

Later that evening, I realized I couldn't possibly be pregnant; this really made me wonder what was going on; what had I been doing? I tried to put everything out of my mind for the evening, but focusing on the movie was a lost cause.

The next day, I went to work very nervous about what all this meant. Prior to all this, a video testimony by the 700 Club kept popping up on my YouTube feed. The title was something about a lady being delivered from the occult. As I was waiting in the parking lot for my shift to start, something told me to watch that video. It was the first one to pop up when I opened YouTube. The lady started talking, and I felt my stomach sink. She was telling my exact story. She grew up abused, started using alcohol and drugs, lived a promiscuous lifestyle, got married, was divorced, and then she started getting involved in the occult.

The difference between our stories was someone told her what she was doing was wrong. They'd even explained why and walked her through deliverance. She recalled in detail how she renounced all her practices and told her "spirit guides" she would no longer be working with them. She said this angered the spirit guides. She then suffered a demonic attack at which point her boyfriend, who was a Holy Spirit-filled Christian, took authority over those unclean spirits and she ceased to suffer. The whole testimony was about five minutes in length, but I felt like time had stopped. In that moment, I needed to decide what to do.

I went to my workstation at a local order fulfillment center where I processed online retail orders. I'd previously received messages in the form of book titles from my "spirit guides" (demons). Before I started working, I verbally said, "I only want to hear from God, Jesus, the Holy Spirit. I don't want to hear from any spirit guides. Am I being deceived?" Within three hours, the first book came through called "The Deceit of Christians." My stomach dropped. I felt panicked. I asked for confirmation and by the end of my shift, I'd received two more book titles confirming my fears. My shift was ten hours long. During this time, my mind was racing. I was in a complete frenzy. It turns out, the demons that were taking up residence inside me were freaking out. I was actually discerning (feeling and knowing) their emotions, but I was so wrapped up in confusion, I thought these were my own feelings.

God gave me so much mercy during this time. He sent the archangel Michael, He prompted me to watch the 700 Club video testimony and on top of all this, He still confirmed my question with three different book titles. I didn't deserve any of this, and I was spared from what I did deserve. This was just the beginning of God showing me His immense, never-ending love.

"For I am persuaded that neither death nor life,

nor angels nor principalities nor powers, nor things present nor things to come, nor height nor depth, nor any other created thing, shall be able to separate us from the love of God which is in Christ Jesus our Lord."

Romans 8:38-39 NKJV

Chapter 7

Renunciation

After work, I went home, renounced witchcraft and took my altar down. I told the spirit guides (demons) that I was only connecting with and honoring Jesus Christ. Within the next few hours, a heavy oppressive spirit made its presence known in my bedroom. It was angry.

The demonic attacks against my family and me started immediately. God also made Himself known. I texted my friend, Joy, and confessed my involvement in the occult. She wasn't Spirit-filled, but immediately knew the implications of what I was telling her. Joy hadn't been able to locate her Bible in the two previous weeks. That night as I texted her, she asked God to reveal where her Bible was. The next day, she told me her Bible appeared on her dresser out of nowhere; even her family was shocked to see it there because she had been looking for it nonstop in the two weeks prior. Joy said that she would pray for me and ask God to be with me.

That same evening, my husband planned to have a daddy/daughter sleepover in our daughter's room. She would sleep in her bed, and he would sleep on the floor until she fell asleep. I was so unsettled in the master bedroom that I asked them both to have their sleepover with me. We crawled into bed, and while my family rested peacefully, I reluctantly closed my eyes.

Later that night, during what is known as the witching hour, I woke up covered in blood. Simultaneously, my daughter woke up screaming. The room was dreadfully cold, even though the heater had been running. Again, I sensed the heavy oppression all through the house and I believe my daughter did too. My husband would later confess to my father that he wasn't sure what happened to us that night, but that he had been scared. Once my husband got our daughter settled in her room, he helped me trash everything in the house related to the occult. There was a set of tarot cards I could not find. I grabbed my husband's hand, prayed a quick prayer asking God to show me where the cards were and I was guided to two Bibles in my room. The deck of cards had fallen behind those two Bibles I hadn't touched in years.

I spent the rest of the night in the guest's bedroom. I didn't sleep at all. I prayed the Lord's prayer over and over. There was one other time I had spent the entire night praying the Lord's prayer repeatedly.

About five years before all this, I bought some psychedelic mushrooms, known as 'shrooms, from my drug dealer. I had never taken 'shrooms before, but with all the previous drugs I had done, I didn't think 'shrooms had much else to offer. I was planning to wait to take them with some friends, but that didn't pan out. I took two and a half times the regular amount I probably should have taken and was tripping on the drugs within thirty minutes.

I started seeing into the spirit realm immediately. At first, it was not bad. I was watching cartoons and letting my mind fade in and out of the altered reality. Eventually, I started seeing demons all over the apartment I was in. This is often referred to as a bad trip.

Wikipedia says "a bad trip (also known as acute intoxication from hallucinogens, psychedelic crisis, or emergence phenomenon) is a frightening and unpleasant experience triggered by psychoactive drugs, especially psychedelic drugs such as LSD and Psilocybin mushroom." Segen's Medical dictionary defines it as a "hallucinogenic drug-induced experience in which the pattern of time-space disorientation causes an intense adverse neuropsychiatric response in the person taking the 'trip'."

It was an awful experience, to say the least. I spent six hours in this bad trip, and the only thing I knew to do was repeat the Lord's prayer over and over.

I experienced the aftershocks of this drug for two weeks. The severity of which spanned from seeing tiny people dancing on a person's desk at work to thinking I was floating. One of the aftershocks I experienced was during a meeting at work. My boss was speaking to me about a marketing campaign we had been working on, but I could not focus because the pattern on his shirt started morphing and dancing. I interrupted him saying I needed to leave and walked out of the meeting without further explanation.

The night of the demonic attack felt very similar to that event, except that day, I had been completely sober. I had not taken any drugs since the night I heard the demons singing to me in unison. That experience freaked me out so much that I was instantly delivered from drug addiction in the natural sense. I had cravings and urges, but those were spiritual implications which would soon be addressed.

Chapter 8

The Pre-Game

The next morning was super bowl Sunday, February 3, 2018. I skipped work and urgently reached out to Linda, one of the only Spirit-filled Christians I knew anymore. I had been texting her since four o'clock in the morning. She told me she could hear the fear in my texts and asked me to meet her at her church the next day.

I found myself at the 11 o'clock service at a local church in New Braunfels, Texas. This was the first time I had been to a church service in over seven years. It felt strange but comforting at the same time. The praise and worship songs were amazing. I felt Holy Spirit ministering to me like He'd never left my side. He hadn't forsaken me through any of the journeys I had been on. He was patiently waiting for His prodigal daughter to return. The

Father greeted me with open arms.

I received guidance and prayer over my daughter and myself from the worship leader. As the worship leader laid his hands on my head, Holy Spirit revealed I had been subjected to multiple hallucinations. He took his hands off me almost as soon as they touched me. He asked about the hallucinations, and I explained I thought they had been "visions". This was the first indication Holy Spirit gave me of being heavily demonized, but neither of us was versed enough in the subject to know the signs. When I got home, I thought the worst was over. I emailed my therapist and canceled all my pre-booked appointments. I felt it extremely important to stop going to therapy immediately.

For the next two months, I immersed myself in the Word. I listened to only Christian music and even fasted a little. I cut out all secular television, except the news and left the world of the occult behind me. God was showing me Christian Apologetics and I was doing as many

Bible studies as I could find on the topics of occult and witchcraft. I wanted to know every word the Bible said about these things so I could repent for everything I'd done.

God also dealt with me severely regarding pride. I had to humble myself to every single Christian person I had misled during my time in the occult and explain the truth to them. The list wasn't long, but it was necessary to right the wrongs by exposing the lies of the enemy. The first people I told were my parents. They kind of already knew I was on the wrong path so the conversation with them wasn't so hard. The follow-up conversations with other people were a little harder. I was called a hypocrite many times, among other things. I lost a friend of twenty years over this, but it was okay because I wanted God's will over my own. I was willing to do whatever was necessary. I had to work out my salvation with fear and trembling (Philippians 2:12).

"Pride goes before destruction, And a haughty spirit before a fall."

Proverbs 16:18 NKJV

"And he gives grace generously. As the Scriptures say, 'God opposes the proud but gives grace to the humble.'"

James 4:6 NLT

During this time, I endured three weeks of hellish nightmares. It was nothing like I had ever experienced before. The nightmares were so awful, I was afraid to sleep by myself. It eventually got to the point where I didn't sleep at all. It was worse than insomnia and I had been dealing with insomnia for twenty years. This was mental torture multiplied exponentially.

I will never forget one dream I had that was so vivid. The dream happened about four years ago, but while writing this book, I suddenly remembered the dream like I'd just had it moments ago. I was in a blue car driving on the highway. The highway approached a bridge. Under the bridge was flowing water. It wasn't particularly fast or slow, but it gave me a sense of peace. As I crossed the bridge, it started to separate and pull apart from itself. The car was right smack in the middle of the separation. Because of this, I thought I was going to fall into the water, but then a huge rock came up out of the water. The car got stuck halfway on the rock and halfway on the part of the bridge that was still in front of me. I couldn't drive the car any longer. I got out of the car and saw the waters starting to rage around me. The waters were rising and I started to feel uneasy thinking I was going to be overtaken, but right before the rock was engulfed, the waters stopped rising. Everything else around me was flooded except for the rock I was on and the part of the bridge behind me.

When I looked to the bridge behind me, a demon was standing there laughing at me. Its laugh cut through me because there was nothing funny about it. It was a hateful, taunting laugh. The demon was about six feet tall, in the form of a disfigured human. Its body was muscular, but its face was rancid. It had a green tint to its skin, its eyes were jet black, its brain was exposed and its teeth were sharpened and pointy on the ends. Its tongue was split like a snake's. It had long arms that were disproportionate to its body. It had a short torso and long legs. For some reason, I remember it was wearing these black shoes that reminded me of steel toe boots. It wasn't wearing a shirt, but it did have on blue jeans that were dirty and ripped.

Standing next to the demon was my therapist. The demon had its arm around her as if it was giving her a side hug. Although she seemed completely unaware of the demon next to her, my therapist was also laughing at me. I felt unbridled fear. I felt trapped. They were the predators and I was the prey. The way they were looking and laughing at me gave me a pit of anxiety in my belly. When I woke from the dream, I was soaked in sweat and my heart was pounding.

At the time of this dream, I didn't have a clear interpretation to know it was nothing to fear. It was God revealing the new path I was on and I was leaving behind the demon that terrorized me. I didn't understand enough about the dream, and I had such an intense physical reaction to it that I was afraid.

I begged God to have mercy on me. I prayed and cried out in tears to please stop the nightmares. I knew He was allowing this to happen to show me something, but I asked Him to show me in a different manner. The nightmares ceased.

"He who conceals his sins does not prosper but whoever confesses and renounces them finds mercy."

Proverbs 28:13 NIV

Through the nightmares, God was revealing to me that I had allowed for partial demonic possession. This is often referred to as demonization. There were parts of my soul so heavily oppressed by the demonic that demon spirits actually had control of me in those areas. When I asked Him to stop the dreams, He had to show me in a different way. This is when the demonic manifestations started happening. I would lose time, lose control of my body, and curse people out, specifically Christians, all without my knowledge of it happening.

By God's grace, Joy told me about a Thursday daytime women's Bible study at the church where I met Linda and received prayer. I started attending those Bible studies. At the second study I attended, I met a woman named Belinda who befriended me. She was younger than me, but had a son the same age as my daughter. We became immediate friends.

One day, a couple of weeks after I met Belinda, she invited me to a park with another friend of hers named Oscar. Belinda knew about my involvement in the occult and mentioned it to Oscar who had deliverance experience. He brought a book with him called *Pigs in the Parlor: A Practical Guide to Deliverance* by Frank Hammond. It was a book I was familiar with and wanted to get but never did because something inside me found it very unsettling. At some point, the subject of occult was brought up and Oscar spoke the truth about it all being satanic.

In the occult, they are very careful to distinguish between the different practices. Green magic is different from sigil magic, which differs from the black arts. When Oscar made mention of biblical truth, my body started getting sick. My stomach started convulsing and I found myself about to throw up. I asked if we could change the subject. The last thing I remember was being bent over some bushes hurling my guts out.

Belinda and Oscar would later reveal a demonic spirit manifested through me. It became belligerent right before I threw up. I had no recollection of this. Oscar said the demonic spirit spoke through me cursing at him and causing a scene.

This was the path God had chosen to show me I was demonized. First, He revealed the hallucinations, then He allowed me to have tormenting nightmares and mental anguish, and last, the demons started manifesting in my physical body.

After we left the park, Belinda and Oscar called me to pray. Collectively we had not cast out anything demonic and I was still suffering attacks. A few days later, Belinda told me her son suffered an attack in the car on their way home from the park. He was sitting in the back seat and started throwing up uncontrollably. Belinda and Oscar pulled over, laid hands on the boy and prayed until he stopped manifesting. I felt terrible.

The next day, I went to the women's Bible study facilitated by a woman named Pastor Sarah. Belinda was there too. As Bible study ended, another woman named Deena approached me offering to help me with spiritual warfare. She invited me to an evening Bible study she hosted with another woman from the church. In the middle of speaking with her, the demonic spirit manifested itself again.

This time, while I was throwing up, the demon got angry because Deena provoked it by asking its name. She started praying in tongues over me, but the demonic spirit, already angry, started mocking her in demonic tongues and swinging my fists at her. After twenty minutes of this, the manifestation stopped. Deena said she would reach out to the leader of her Bible study so they could help me. Later that day, Deena's grandmother would suffer a demonic attack.

Deena's grandma was living in Washington State, I believe. She was in her nineties and in a nursing home. After what had happened to me, I recall Deena saying she went to Pastor Sarah to get prayer. As she left the church, she received several phone calls from her dad. He told Deena her grandma started violently throwing up blood and had been taken to the hospital because they didn't know what was causing it. Deena, upon hearing this news, pulled her vehicle over and immediately started interceding.

Deena was suffering from Matthew 12:43-45 (NIV), except in a different manner. Her family was now being attacked. Deena told me her grandma's ordeal lasted about two hours. The vomiting stopped and the doctors never knew what caused it. This happened because Deena had provoked the spirit until it had manifested, but she had not prayed me through a complete deliverance. She poked the bear and it came back with its friends. The same thing happened to Belinda, Oscar and her son the day before. They unknowingly provoked the demonic spirit inside me to manifest itself, but they didn't complete the deliverance.

A few days later, Deena told me I had a soul tie with the devil and these women who'd initially offered to help me wouldn't come near me. A rumor was also started that I had sold my soul to Satan. It brought sadness to my heart to hear these things about me because these people didn't know me. I didn't knowingly choose to become a slave to Satan or a home to his demonic minions. I originally thought they were under the influence of a spirit of gossip and it only brought further condemnation to what I was already experiencing.

After healing from this experience, Holy Spirit revealed a big lesson to me. The enemy perverted someone's fear and unfamiliarity by taking advantage of it. What I thought was gossip was just another person trying to seek out the heart of God in order to help me. Only God can judge the intent of the heart. It is our job to discern it. One reason people shy away from deliverance is because of situations like this one. They fear gossip, judgment and rejection. It is important for the oppressed person to understand that total reliance on God is essential. It will cause an oppressed person to move forward in their healing and deliverance process despite the enemy's tricks.

Deena stayed connected with me for the next few weeks to make sure I was reading the Bible. She would reach out to me a few times a week via text to make sure I was in the Word, and she was trying to teach me how to fight on my own, but beyond that, I felt terribly forgotten. Isolation is another tactic of the enemy, but I was so desperate for deliverance, I would not stop seeking it.

When I realized I was demonized, I was absolutely destroyed. The only thing I knew to do was trust God through the process, which turned out to be long. I wanted to be purified in an instant, but I needed to grow my spirit man. I had to feed myself. I had to come, taste and see that God is good.

"Taste and see that the Lord is good; blessed is the one who takes refuge in him."

Psalms 34:8 NIV

About a month prior to the first demonic manifestation, I'd asked Pastor Sarah who I could go to for spiritual warfare. She said I should talk to Pat Mendoza. Pat was an elder of the local church. During each service, she translated in American Sign Language for the congregation. She was there every Sunday and the first Wednesday of the church's only night services. This was all I knew about her.

I had just missed the first Wednesday of the month's night service, and since I worked weekends, I had not been able to meet with Pat during the weekend. I knew that if I could make it to the Wednesday night church service that was to take place in three weeks, Pat would be my best bet. It is critical to understand the desperation I was under at this point. The mental anguish I was experiencing was absolutely horrifying. Every day I had to battle for my sanity. My husband worked away from home and my daughter was in school. I was home alone all day being tormented by demons.

I was fully aware of what the demonic spirits could do because of what I had given them access to in my life. While I was in the occult, I had many different supernatural experiences. One day, I had come home from the grocery store. I bought my daughter a helium-filled balloon and left it in the living room for her to have when she got home from school. While I was doing my daily cleaning, the balloon started moving around the house. It was being pushed from room to room. I didn't notice at first because it was slowly moving and I was busy with laundry, cooking and other chores. It wasn't until I went to the hallway and ran into the string tied to the balloon that I realized it had moved. I put it back in the living room. The next time I noticed it, it was in the front foyer. The air condition wasn't on and the windows weren't open. It was particularly intriguing because the rooms had archways through which the balloon had to pass. The balloon would have to dip at least half a foot to clear the archways in order to be moved from room to room.

I knew what was going on and I was humored. I tied the balloon to a lamp in the living room and it started spinning in a full circle kind of like it was orbiting something. I spoke up saying, "I get it. I know what you're doing, but this is starting to freak me out. Please stop." The balloon stopped spinning instantly.

Another time, I had recited an incantation to a "god of bees" and when I opened the back door to my house, a bee flew inside. It wasn't a bumble bee or wasp, it was a bee I had never seen before. It followed me around the house and would gently buzz around me as if to play. After I tired of the buzzing, I opened the front door of my house and told the bee to leave. It flew out immediately.

In addition to these minor interactions, demonic spirits in other people would make themselves known to me often. In particular, the spirit of autism wanted to be known. This happened three different times with three different people. The first time it happened was at work. A coworker I never engaged with came up to me and started telling me he was autistic. He never spoke with anyone; his work was uniquely designed so that he didn't have to talk to anyone. I knew it was a manifestation. It told me in specific detail that the autism these people suffered was spiritual oppression and generational.

AutismSpeaks.org writes, "Autism, or autism spectrum disorder (ASD), refers to a broad range of conditions characterized by challenges with social skills, repetitive behaviors, speech and nonverbal communication. According to the Centers for Disease Control, autism affects an estimated 1 in 54 children in the United States today."

The site goes on to say the spectrum of autism is influenced by both environmental and genetic elements. People with autism experience sensory issues typically with sensitivities to external stimuli. It is also associated with certain physical and mental conditions. Until recently, the general consensus was that autism could not be cured, only treated. It is now generally believed that those with the diagnosis can possibly outgrow the condition.

The second time I encountered the spirit of autism, it told me the boy it had afflicted was under its oppression because he had been misdiagnosed. The demon said the boy's

Christian mother continually spoke the misdiagnosis over her son. The spirit confirmed the power of death and life in our tongues.

"Death and life are in the power of the tongue, And those who love it will eat its fruit."

Proverbs 18:21 NKJV

After I renounced the occult, my interactions were more severe. I had come home from the gym one day, and while I was in the shower, a bar of soap flew off the soap holder full force at my head. I just happened to duck in time for it to miss. It banged against the glass wall and fell to the floor. After that I kept everything in the shower on the floor, just in case.

During this time, I hardly slept. Every night, I would feel the oppressive spirit come into my room and just be there watching me. I would see demons during the day, especially at my house. Sometimes, out of pure exhaustion, I would take a nap during the day, and when I would wake up, there would be demons standing around the bed looking at me. It was nerve-racking. I would feel them behind me, following me around the house. They would flick and pull at my hair. They would try to push me into things or make me trip as I would walk.

When I went outside to work on the yard, I would find small dead animals around the house. I was being bullied by demons. That's not something you tend to tell a lot of people. I could hear and see them, so my main task in drowning them out was to keep my focus on God and His Word. I played Christian music in my house nonstop, even throughout the night. I did what I knew to do and waited on God's timing for the rest.

I did try to go to other churches in the area for help, but every time I'd pass a church, Holy Spirit would give me an emphatic NO. That one specific local church turned into this beacon of light for me, and I didn't know or understand why until I met Pat in person.

I finally made it to Wednesday. It was April 4, 2018. The entire day was filled with anxiety and torment. I was throwing up, I was fevered, I was exhausted. I didn't know what to expect that evening. I picked my three-year old daughter up from preschool, fed her and got us ready for church. As soon as we got to the sanctuary, my daughter started acting out. I tried to leave the service early, but I literally could not walk to the front doors. I would find myself in the lobby several times, about ten feet from the doors, but I couldn't go any further. I eventually hunkered down in the cry room until service was over. I was feeling extremely anxious, but had no idea why. After the service ended, I hunted down Pat who I only knew as the woman who did sign language.

Chapter 9

Deliverance

Pat was a short Hispanic woman with short black hair. She had a warm glance in her eyes and a calm demeanor. She wore modest jewelry, a red shirt with a black belt, black slacks and black pumps for shoes. She had a particularly spectacular smile. It was genuine and caring. I watched her greet other members of the church and I waited impatiently while she made pleasantries. I interrupted one conversation, too anxious to wait my turn. I thought I greeted her politely asking, "Hi, are you Pat Mendoza?" Later Holy Spirit would reveal to me that my approach was more aggressive and accusatory as if to question "Who do you think you are?" This was a demonic manifestation.

As soon as I met Pat, I could feel the anointing of the Holy Spirit on her. I was drawn to her like a moth to a flame. I remember telling her I had left the occult and I really needed help and prayer in spiritual warfare. I told her I'd manifested and scared some other church members, at which point Pat gave me a huge grandmotherly smile and said, "Well, that's okay because I FEAR NO EVIL." At the prompting of Holy Spirit, she offered me her number and to pray with me. I thought it odd that she was taking off her shoes and pushing up her shirtsleeves like she was about to go into a fight. Later I'd find out Holy Spirit was telling her to provoke the spirits within me by giving me her number and offering to pray for me.

I didn't speak to her for more than a minute before the demonic spirits manifested for the final time. My stomach started convulsing and I started throwing up on the floor of the sanctuary. Pat put one hand on my stomach and one hand on my neck, bent me over and started deliverance on me.

Tears, mucus, and spit spewed from the

openings of my face. I couldn't see a whole lot happening, but I could hear everything. The next day, God revealed to me that I had thrown up some copious amounts of blood and black tar stuff. I remember things like Pat casting out the demonic spirits with a very fearless and fierce authority in Christ. She didn't yell. She mostly spoke directly into my ear almost in an authoritative whisper enforcing demonic eviction.

The event took many of the church members by surprise. There were still a handful of people in the sanctuary when I started manifesting. I do recall seeing maybe five or six people standing in a circle around me in addition to Pat and her husband, David. They were praying in the Spirit while Pat continued to exercise her authority in Christ.

In the middle of a reprieve, I looked around for my daughter. David had taken her to another church member for safe oversight. My daughter was giggling profusely at the woman she was with. She had no idea what was going on outside of her and her new friend because her attention was fully engaged away from what was happening with me. God was truly covering my daughter.

I remember speaking in my voice in English, crying out for Jesus and speaking in tongues against the demon. I also remember the demon mocking Pat in laughter and demonic tongues. I could literally feel the Holy Spirit inside me fighting the demonic entity. It is one thing to know and feel the manifested presence of God around you. It is a whole different thing to feel God's manifested presence INSIDE you.

Pat continued to command the demonic spirits to leave. When they manifested in anger, she laughed at them. More than halfway into the deliverance, a demonic spirit tried to lift Pat off my body. She had been crouched over me, as if to cradle my body while I was throwing up and convulsing. She handled me with gentleness until the demon tried to get her away from me. I felt a supernatural strength rise up from my core. Pat laid on top of me and

I felt the full weight of her body trying to keep my body pinned in submission. This ordeal lasted for 45 minutes.

I finally stopped throwing up the black tar. Pat wiped my face clean with a wet towel. She helped me up off the ground and told me they were gone. I exhaled with relief and a bit of gladness. I had a heavy haze over my eyes that made everything look fuzzy. I remember asking if something was wrong with my eyes because I couldn't see normally. I was seeing the heavenly spirit realm around us, I didn't know this at that time. I was seeing into the supernatural realm of angels and heavenly creatures. I could see the essence of trees and animals in such a way I'd never experienced before.

This intense gaze into the spirit realm lasted about two weeks. I still see in the spirit, but not nearly as intensely. Over time, God would continue to give me insight into the night I got delivered. He showed me how right before Pat laid hands on my stomach, the entire sanctuary was flooded with an angelic army of heavenly hosts. I remember feeling the atmosphere change with the charge of the angelic presence.

"It was revealed to them that they were not serving themselves but you, when they spoke of the things that have now been told you by those who have preached the gospel to you by the Holy Spirit sent from heaven. EVEN ANGELS LONG TO LOOK INTO THESE THINGS."

1 Peter 1:12 NIV, emphasis added.

The next day I was exhausted and tired, but free. ENTIRELY FREE. I could feel the freeness. I wasn't fighting anger and bitterness anymore. I wasn't frightened. I was delivered by God's perfect mercy. Years of addiction, abuse, and condemnation were broken off me. I was finally walking free. The fight had just begun.

"And we know that in all things God works for the good of those who love him who have been called according to his purpose."

Romans 8:28 NIV

Chapter 10

Maintaining Deliverance

The thing no one mentions about generational curses and demonic bondage is that they are so much easier to break off the bloodline compared to the work it takes to change the habitual behavior instilled while growing up. Breaking generational curses and maintaining this freedom takes intentional work by changing one's behavior.

Since experiencing deliverance from the occult in 2018, I have maintained my deliverance because my life depends on it. I want my children and my children's children to walk in freedom. I want freedom to be passed through our bloodlines because generational blessings are also biblical.

"The Lord said to Jehu, 'Because you have done well in accomplishing what is right in my eyes and have done to the house of Ahab all I had in mind to do, your descendants will sit on the throne of Israel to the fourth generation.'"

2 Kings 10:30 NIV

One of the first things I did in preparation for freedom was consecrate myself. Consecrate means to make holy or to dedicate to a higher purpose. "The 'secr' part of consecrate comes from the Latin sacer meaning 'sacred'". It can be said that something consecrated is dedicated to God and is therefore sacred (Source: Vocabulary.com).

"But know that the Lord has set apart for Himself him who is godly; The Lord will hear when I call to Him."

Psalms 4:3 NKJV

Being set apart and consecrated has been of high importance in maintaining deliverance. I don't drink, do drugs or go to bars or clubs. I don't even sit near the bar when I go to a restaurant. I guard my eyes, ears, tongue, and heart fiercely. I do not watch the news, I rarely watch TV and I surely do not go to the movies. I rarely listen to secular music. If I do, it's classical or country music. I limit my time on social media to less than twenty minutes a day for all platforms, unless it relates to edifying my spirit. I refuse to listen to or watch anything that would take my focus off God. Holy Spirit has continuously given me guidelines as to what I should or should not do. This type of consecration is not for everyone, but it works very well for me.

"And do not be conformed to this world, but be transformed by the renewing of your mind, that you may prove what is that good and acceptable and perfect will of God."

Romans 12:2 NKJV

"All things are lawful for me, but not all things are helpful; all things are lawful for me, but not all things edify."

I Corinthians 10:23 NKJV

In addition to separating myself from the world, I had to learn to pour into myself and my relationship with God. If I'm taking myself out of the world, but not putting myself in the Lord, it becomes legalistic and pointless. This is how religion operates. Relationship is different. I spend time with God daily. Praying is second nature to me because it is just talking to God, and I talk to Him about everything. I have heard people teach that God is all-knowing and all-powerful, so why concern Him with the little things in life, like "What do I eat today?" However, that is exactly what my relationship with Him is like. I concern Him with everything, just like little kids do with their parents. He is my Father and there hasn't been one thing I've concerned Him with that He's turned His attention away from.

Then there are times that I sit quietly and listen. Sometimes, this is a little harder because, like a kid, I can be impatient to hear my Father's voice. Thankfully, He left a huge book full of His voice. I crave being in the Word of God and knowing His will. I took very practical steps to get in the Word daily. I posted index cards and notes all over my house full of scriptures and prayers. I unwittingly began to memorize scriptures from doing this. On the front, I would write a verse, and on the back, I would write a corresponding prayer. When people would visit me, I would often be led to share these scripture and prayer cards with them. I was evangelizing and didn't even know it.

Even when I don't feel like it, I ask God to manifest His will in the lives of my family and myself. I praise and worship Him often. Changing negative behaviors then easily becomes a direct result of having a relationship with Jesus. We must desire Him so much that we start and end our days with Him.

"And when He had sent the multitudes away, He went up on the mountain by Himself to pray. Now when evening came, He was alone there."
                                                    Matthew 14:23 NKJV

Praying in the Holy Spirit is also vitally important. Believers baptized in the Spirit must start praying in the Holy Spirit more. What is it like being able to pray in the Spirit and not actually do it? God said it's like having a stack of books by your favorite author, but never reading them. You have access to unlimited knowledge and wisdom if you just took the time to sit down and read the book (pray in the Holy Spirit). Unfortunately, many believers don't. After I was delivered, Holy Spirit pressed upon me to pray in the Spirit more. I started with about an hour a day. Eventually, I was praying in the Holy Spirit over ten hours a day. I understand not everyone will have the unction to pray that long, but every little bit counts. Not a day goes by that I don't pray in the Spirit for at least fifteen minutes.

Pray without ceasing. It is a commandment, albeit not one of the Ten Commandments, but a command nonetheless, and it is God's will for us.

"Rejoice always, pray without ceasing, in everything give thanks; for this is the will of God in Christ Jesus for you."

I Thessalonians 5:16-18 NKJV

Holy Spirit gives us utterances and helps us pray. Praying without ceasing is easy when you pray in the Spirit. I would pray everywhere. If I wasn't speaking to someone in English, I was praying in the Spirit.

And they were all filled with the Holy Spirit and began to speak with other tongues, as the Spirit gave them utterance."

Acts 2:4 NKJV

"Likewise the Spirit also helps in our weaknesses. For we do not know what we should pray for as we ought, but the Spirit Himself makes intercession for us with groanings which cannot be uttered."

Romans 8:26 NKJV

Additionally, I am accountable. Finding a truly sanctified person to be accountable to came two and a half years after I left the occult. We talk daily. She laughs with me, cries with me, believes with me. We don't battle together because our victory is already won, but she stands with me, and when I need it the most, she prays with and for my family and me. Her name is Carolina. I could not ask for a truer friend in the natural. She loves me enough to tell me the truth of God's Word even when she knows it will cause me some pain. Pain doesn't have to hurt, but when it does, I love her enough to talk to her the next day. She is not just a Christian friend, her friendship with me is for the purpose of the God's Kingdom. It has been divinely ordained by God.

Christian friendships do not automatically translate to accountability in relationships. When finding someone to be accountable to, it should be someone we trust and respect. Not everyone has the spiritual maturity or is willing to hold you accountable to biblical standards. We will know them by their fruit. Do they actually sharpen our iron and give us biblical correction out of love, or is it all just fluff?

"Therefore, putting away lying, "Let each one of you speak truth with his neighbor," for we are members of one another."

Ephesians 4:25 NKJV

We should come to a keen understanding of our identities in Christ. It comes with power and authority in Him. We are spiritual beings having a human experience. Angels and demons will never have the human experience. They will only ever experience the supernatural in their spirit form. This could be why angels look into such things and demons want to be in possession of our souls. I spent hours upon hours in Galatians, Ephesians, Colossians and Romans, which are all books that tell us how to live our lives as Christians. These books, along with the Bible as a whole, explain the power and authority that Jesus gave us when He rose from the dead. The enemy absolutely does not want us to know our power and authority. When we walk in this knowledge and exercise our power and authority in Jesus Christ, the kingdom of darkness is shaken and the enemy trembles.

Above all else, I live a life of submission and obedience to God because I love Him. I have a relationship with Father, Son, Holy Spirit. My Father is my Lord, Jesus is my Savior and Holy

Spirit is my Best Friend. I repent at the first sign of grieving Him. I fellowship with Him daily. This includes deliberate prayer, intercession, praying in tongues and fasting when called to. Mostly, I just talk to Him, and most importantly, I listen in submission. I would be dead in the spirit and possibly in the natural if it weren't for God.

We should learn to take spiritual inventory of our families. The same way we look at natural ailments is how we should be treating spiritual ailments. When we go to our doctors, they ask if depression runs in our families, if someone is hypertensive, if anyone has cancer, and so forth. We are our own best advocates, and digging into the spiritual inventory of our families, both paternal and maternal, can reveal a multitude of curses that need to be broken. If we don't have access to our parents, we can ask aunts, uncles or cousins. Holy Spirit will also help. He will delightfully reveal these things to those who want to know.

"But the Helper, the Holy Spirit, whom the

Father will send in My name, He will teach you all things, and bring to your remembrance all things that I said to you."

John 14:26 NKJV

Repent often and receive forgiveness. I try to stay in submission and repentance; this is so that I remain in the Father's will and receive His forgiveness when I step outside of His bounds. For about two years after the deliverance event at the church, whenever I found myself around anything dealing remotely with the occult, I would purge the atmosphere by throwing up. I did this so often that I thought I was going to be throwing up for the rest of my life when discerning things of the occult. The same thing would happen when I would repent and ask God to cleanse me of anything not of Him. I would start to get this nauseous feeling, and I would eventually purge my body.

In the last six months prior to writing this book, I have come to be able to purge the atmosphere and myself much less intrusively. It comes from having a heart of submission to

God. I asked Holy Spirit to teach me how to cleanse the atmosphere and myself without throwing up. I still have feelings of nausea, but I can now expel demons from the atmosphere and myself simply by telling them to go and/or exhaling them away. I also have a much better understanding of how I discern the occult, which has helped me navigate certain situations a lot better and with more wisdom.

Not long ago, I met a woman named Samantha. She is a farmer in the community where I live. I stopped by her farm one day to pick up some groceries for dinner. When I walked up to Samantha to greet her, I started feeling nauseous. I knew she had some type of occultic demon oppressing her. The longer I talked to her, the more my stomach turned. It was uncomfortable like when you have a splinter, but it wasn't terribly unbearable. I asked Holy Spirit what to do and He said to minister to her through a word of knowledge. I shared with her what He told me and I could see that it blessed her. In the past, I might have done something foolish like tried to confront the demon. In this case, all I needed to do was listen to Holy Spirit. My relationship with Him fostered a loving response to an otherwise uncomfortable situation.

Take communion regularly. At the start of writing this book, spiders started showing up inside my RV. I live on twenty acres of land inside an RV. The RV is parked next to an uncleared part of the land that is full of wildlife and overgrown trees. Finding bugs inside is par for the course, however, we were only finding spiders and it was more than usual. First, it was one, then two, then more and more as the days progressed. They even started showing up in my car. At the prompting of my six-year old, we took communion twice—once before bed and when we woke up. The spiders ceased to show any longer. Sometimes, it isn't just us to be reminded that we belong to God and what Jesus did for us on the cross. Sometimes, the enemy needs to have it shoved in his face that we have the victory over him.

We should anoint our homes and our physical bodies often. I go through seasons when I know I need to anoint my home or myself, be it my eyes, ears or mind. In doing so, I have asked God to redeem the gifts He has given me. There is no room for the enemy in my life because I have asked God to be God over all things. Anointing our homes also gives notice to the enemy that he is not welcome, and it creates a hedge of protection.

"And you shall take the anointing oil, pour it on his head, and anoint him."

Exodus 29:7 NKJV

"But you, when you fast, anoint your head and wash your face,"

Matthew 6:17 NKJV

I have asked Holy Spirit to help me stay sober-minded and vigilant. The enemy is sneaky and conniving. Discerning an attack by the help of Holy Spirit is crucial to our spiritual health. He helps us become more aware of patterns and triggers.

"Be sober, be vigilant; because your adversary the devil walks about like a roaring lion, seeking whom he may devour."

I Peter 5:8 NKJV

Offense is a great example for me. Walking in offense was like second nature to me. The wind would blow wrong and I would manage to find some type of offense in that. It was like I was in a perpetual state of offense because that is how I learned to be growing up. I had to consciously identify the feeling that would come and then submit it to God.

"Prepare the table, Set a watchman in the tower, Eat and drink. Arise, you princes, Anoint the shield!"

Isaiah 21:5 NKJV

Speaking of feelings, we cannot allow ourselves to be controlled by our emotions. This was another area that I needed to submit to the Word. At the writing of this book, I am still being healed in the area of my emotions, but I have taken strides upon strides in the right direction.

Trust in the Lord. When we begin to learn and discern His will for our lives, we can then move forward with less friction in the spirit. Sometimes, this can be uncomfortable, but other times, it can be a breeze. I was driving around our property one time when these two grasshoppers landed on the hood of my vehicle. I was approaching about twenty miles per hour. One was facing me so its back was to the wind. The other was facing forward towards the direction I was driving in and it was hanging on for dear life. Its little antennas were bent backwards and it seemed dreadfully uncomfortable. When we let God take control, it is best to look at Him and not worry about where we are going because, whether we can see it or not, we will get there. If we are like the grasshopper facing the direction of the winds, we might get there hanging on for dear life all because we have to see what's coming.

"Trust in the Lord with all your heart, And lean not on your own understanding."

Proverbs 3:5 NKJV

Other times, we have to get uncomfortable to know we are in God's will. We can be like Moses who had a stuttering problem, Ezekiel who had to lay on his side for over 400 days or Esther who had to approach an unapproach-able king. When God says to do something, He will provide the way. Just because it's uncom-fortable doesn't mean it isn't God. Being com-fortable means being familiar. We tend to gravi-tate to these things because it is a lot easier than going outside our comfort zones. Walking with God means being comfortable outside of your comfort zone. Writing this book at the lev-el of transparency God is requiring is extremely uncomfortable, but I know it is God's will. I also know His plans for me far exceed any plans I might have for myself.

"For as the heavens are higher than the earth, So are My ways higher than your ways, And My thoughts than your thoughts."

Isaiah 55:9 NKJV

Do not stay isolated. In chapter eight, I briefly
commented that the enemy was using isolation
as another tactic to keep me bound. It is an approach the enemy will use over and over to
keep us blind. Why is isolation so effective?
Because in isolation, we don't have anyone to
help lift up our arms when we grow weary during the battle.

"Now Amalek came and fought with Israel in
Rephidim. And Moses said to Joshua, "Choose
us some men and go out, fight with Amalek.
Tomorrow I will stand on the top of the hill with
the rod of God in my hand." So Joshua did as
Moses said to him, and fought with Amalek.
And Moses, Aaron, and Hur went up to the top
of the hill. And so it was, when Moses held up
his hand, that Israel prevailed; and when he let
down his hand, Amalek prevailed. But Moses'
hands became heavy; so they took a stone and
put it under him, and he sat on it. And Aaron
and Hur supported his hands, one on one side,
and the other on the other side; and his hands

were steady until the going down of the sun.
So Joshua defeated Amalek and his people
with the edge of the sword."

Exodus 17:8-13 NKJV

The enemy's tactics are nothing new. What
does the pandemic of 2020 have in common
with the Biblical story of Elijah in a cave?
Isolation. The pandemic resulted in worldwide
lockdowns and created mass isolation. My
youngest daughter, Noah, was born during this
time. When I was in the hospital ready to give
birth, I couldn't leave my room, and the only
person allowed to visit me at the hospital was
my husband. After we took Noah home, she
didn't meet anyone from our extended families
until she was three months old because
everyone was afraid to get her sick. My
husband and I didn't share these concerns, but
we understood why people were cautious.

I went to a vocational Bible school play for my
oldest daughter, Luna, when Noah was one
and a half years old. The auditorium was full of
kids from preschool age to high school age.

Parents packed the pews to watch the show. Noah was in awe, and a woman sitting close by noticed Noah's mixed expressions of wonder and trepidation. The lady asked if Noah was born during the pandemic, and I confirmed. She noted, "You know, I was reading an article the other day about a whole generation being born into isolation because of the pandemic. I never thought of it that way." I then looked up at a young girl on stage and noticed her shirt. It said:

I survived:

A pandemic

Lockdowns

Virtual school

Snowmageddon (when the entire state of Texas was most notably covered in many feet of snow, along with the majority of the country.)

Days without power and electricity (during Snowmageddon).

Many people would argue that this wasn't the doing of the enemy, but given the severity of the situation, I believe that there were demonic influences behind that entire season of isolation. The enemy would stop at nothing to isolate people and keep them from being in close physical proximity to other people.

"How could one chase a thousand, And two put ten thousand to flight, Unless their Rock had sold them, And the Lord had surrendered them?"

Deuteronomy 32:30 NKJV

Compare this to Elisha going into a cave:
"And Ahab told Jezebel all that Elijah had done, also how he had executed all the prophets with the sword. Then Jezebel sent a messenger to Elijah, saying, "So let the gods do to me, and more also, if I do not make your life as the life of one of them by tomorrow about this time." And when he saw that, he arose and ran for his life, and went to Beersheba, which belongs to Judah, and left his servant there. But he himself went a day's journey into the wilderness, and came and sat down under a broom tree. And he prayed that he might die, and said, "It is enough! Now, Lord, take my life, for I am no better than my fathers!""

I Kings 19:1-4 NKJV

One of the most powerful and prolific prophets of the Old Testament was scared into isolation and wanted to die! He didn't have anyone to encourage or lift him up out of depression, so God Himself visited Elijah to break the spiritual bondage he was in.

"And he said, 'I have been very zealous for the Lord God of hosts; because the children of Israel have forsaken Your covenant, torn down Your altars, and killed Your prophets with the sword. I alone am left; and they seek to take my life.' Then the Lord said to him: 'Go, return on your way to the Wilderness of Damascus; and when you arrive, anoint Hazael as king over Syria. Also you shall anoint Jehu the son of Nimshi as king over Israel. And Elisha the son of Shaphat of Abel Meholah you shall anoint as prophet in your place. It shall be that whoever escapes the sword of Hazael, Jehu will kill; and whoever escapes the sword of Jehu, Elisha will kill. Yet I have reserved seven thousand in Israel, all whose knees have not

134

bowed to Baal, and every mouth that has not kissed him.'"

I Kings 19:14-18 NKJV

We need to thoroughly prepare for deliverance and healing. There is a difference between doing something out of paranoia and doing something out of preparation.

The word prepare is found 159 times in the Old and New Testament.

"Prepare your outside work, Make it fit for yourself in the field; And afterward build your house."

Proverbs 24:27 NKJV

Prepare means being willing to do something or make something ready for use or consideration. God gives us ample instruction and time to prepare ourselves as living sacrifices and freewill offerings to Him. We need to be willing to offer ourselves to Him and to make ourselves ready for His use.

The enemy will sneak up on us no matter what. He is always looking for an opportunity to catch us off guard, and for this reason, we need to be prepared. This reminds me of an experience I had the first time I went scuba diving in the open ocean. I had gotten my scuba diving license in south Texas. The only places to go for my field hours were lakes. The first time I had a series of open ocean dives had taken place off the coast of Belize. Every single thing that could go wrong went wrong on every single dive. The first dive was a night dive. I was given Dawn soap to rub inside my goggles, which helps prevent foggy buildup. In my haste, I didn't rinse the soap out well enough, and this ended with the soap burning my eyes. Also on this dive, another inexperienced diver got too close to me and kicked my regulator (used for breathing precious oxygen) out of my mouth.

On another dive, the camera I had with me got tangled around both my regulator and secondary hoses. Someone grabbed the camera from me not knowing the strap was tangled around my equipment, and subsequently snatched all my breathing hoses out of my mouth and away from my grasp. I believe we were fifty feet deep and I was swallowing nothing but ocean water. The divemaster quickly shoved his secondary breathing hose into my mouth and I regained my composure. On yet another dive, at ninety feet, one of the hoses to my oxygen tanks wasn't tightened properly so my tank began to lose air quickly. I looked down at my pressure gauge and realized I would be out of air within a few minutes because of how fast the air was leaking. I thought for a second that I could panic or I could just relax and wait for someone from my group to meet up with me. I decided to sit at the bottom of the ocean floor and wait. Not long after, a couple from my group came down to me. They noticed the bubbles coming from my tank and motioned if I needed help. They gave me a secondary regulator and swam with me at intervals back to the surface. Thankfully, all the lake training I've received prepared me for every single situation that went wrong. I had a choice to give in to the feelings of panic or rely on my training.

Lastly, we need to stop entertaining demons. This was something Pat told me almost daily. It took me about six weeks to fully grasp what she meant. I understood the words she was saying, but I didn't know how to put it into practice. I had become so accustomed to their presence in my life that I was still giving them power by recognizing that they were still around.

"Submit yourselves therefore to God. Resist the devil, and he will flee from you."

James 4:7 KJV

This scripture is so interesting to me and is very key to figuring out how to stop entertaining demonic spirits. Apostle Bryan Meadows has a teaching on this scripture, and he talks specifically about the word "flee". He teaches that the word is the equivalent of saying a dog will run away with its tail tucked between its legs. When I heard this teaching and specifically the meaning of that word in its original context, I felt very empowered. I was already submitting to God. The enemy had no choice but to flee because I started magnifying the Lord in my life and I stopped magnifying the demonic. This is a direct result of genuine repentance, praise and worship. The day the lightbulb turned on regarding the words to "stop entertaining demons," I called Pat with such excitement. It is such a simple concept, but it took me some time to realize my focus needed a course correction.

Chapter 11

Healing Within Deliverance

Deliverance should not be traumatic. If it is, this could only mean that there is still healing that needs to happen. The healing is a form of God's love for us. The initial breaking is not always traumatic, but sometimes, the digging and resurfacing of what needs healing can be traumatizing if not correctly dealt with. The process has to be intentional. When we are being delivered, it is happening because we are willing to put in the work to be fully healed.

Take a broken nose, for example. An accidental bat to the nose during a game of softball would cause some major damage. Chances are, there would be so much adrenaline from the impact that the person hit by the bat would likely not experience much pain. There would probably be some soreness, swelling and bruising through the healing

process, but once it was over, it would be
forgotten about. Six weeks later, an underlying
issue with breathing could be discovered, and
this issue would be traced back to the initial
accident. This would mean that the nose hadn't
healed properly from the initial trauma. If the
nose isn't fixed, this could lead to having a
crooked nose for life (outward issues) or long-
term breathing problems (inward issues). A
doctor would then decide that the nose has to
be broken again in order to set it so that it
could heal properly.

This time, there would be anticipation building
up to the surgery because there would be full
awareness of what was coming and what is to
be expected. The initial accident happened
quickly; there had been some pain that
surfaced through the three-week healing
process, but it was forgotten. Now there would
be a hospital, surgery, follow-up appointments
and medical bills involved. The memory of the
pain would also resurface. All these factors can
be discouraging and traumatizing, but the
person making the decision to get their nose

fixed would have to be intentional about going through the necessary steps to be properly healed. This means that the person would have to take accountability for scheduling the surgery, going to the hospital, participating in follow-up appointments, and paying the medical bills.

Deliverance isn't just realizing that parts of your soul and spirit were accidentally or even intentionally broken at one point, it is acknowledging that they didn't heal properly. God is the doctor saying, "This isn't right and it is causing long-term damage. We need to fix this, but I need you to do your part and schedule the surgery by coming to the hospital, going to the follow-up appointments and paying the medical bills!" No one has to stay bound. Long-term healing is everyone's portion.

"Therefore if the Son makes you free, you shall be free indeed."

John 8:36 NKJV

One of the sweetest things I experienced while

writing this book is remembering the different stages of healing I have been through. This is also essential to maintaining deliverance. After deliverance, it is no longer about reopening the wound, it's remembering the scar. Earlier in chapter two, I expressed how I had forgotten everything I had already been delivered from. I didn't walk out the full deliverance through complete healing, which is what I have been doing this time for the past four years. God pours out His love every time I heal and remember what He has done for me. It has been surreal and magnificent.

Furthermore, as I continue to heal, I continue to embrace all stages of my life, past and present. It has also allowed me to look to the future with excitement for what is to come. In chasing God's heart and will for my life, I have inevitably sought after healing with a passion. Healing from spiritual wounds is absolutely essential to maintaining deliverance. We can cast out all the demons we want, but if we don't heal, we are just another target for oppression.

How do we maintain deliverance by healing from wounds? This goes back to changing habitual behaviors learned over time. An abused person knows how to abuse, but they have to learn to love. The fruit of the Spirit will manifest when the Spirit is present, but you also have to crucify the flesh and CHOOSE the fruit.

Be disciplined! The enemy's patience can outpace one's undisciplined obedience. We should be intentional about doing what God has asked us to do.

"If you are willing and obedient, You shall eat the good of the land."

Isaiah 1:19 NKJV

Be careful not to seek to be in control. Control is fear based. Rather, seek order because God is a God of order.

"For God is not a God of disorder but of peace – as in all the congregations of the Lord's people."

1 Corinthians 14:33 NIV

Order comes from love. Control will lead to oppression, but order will set the captives free. Order and control clash with each other because control is the perversion of order. We usually think chaos is the perversion of order, but it isn't. People try to control chaos when in reality, chaos needs to be set in order. Chaos can be affected by either control or order, but it is the motive behind it that matters. Is there an attempt to control something because it is being done out of fear, or is there order because God is in the midst of a thing?

Honor the people who have offended you. I NEVER thought I would have reconciled my relationships with my parents. Over twenty years ago, my spiritual mom at the time prophesied to me that I would be the person to lead my dad to a relationship with Jesus. Through the years, I wrestled with the prophecy. I knew it was true, but I had no idea how God was going to bring it to pass. Even when I was in the occult, I would experience visions of laying hands on my dad. It wasn't unreasonable to think that God was still speaking to me during that time because He never leaves us nor forsakes us.

I received the vision of the future one day when I was at work. I was sober, talking to demons when I suddenly saw my hands placed on my dad's shoulder. In the vision, my dad was sitting down. I was standing next to him and I was praying. I was asking Holy Spirit to come upon my dad. The vision ended. My honest and immediate reaction was to laugh out loud. My second reaction was to say verbally, "Joke's on You, I don't even talk to my dad." Within a week of that vision, my dad and I had our first conversation together after two years of not talking. This is when I began to share things of the occult with him.

After I was delivered and began to immerse myself in the Word, I built up my spirit to the point that I started ministering the Word to my dad. On May 16th, 2018, my dad received salvation in the comfort of his home. On June

20th, 2018, my dad was baptized in the Holy
Spirit. My dad had been the source of so much
pain and abuse throughout my childhood, and
there I was laying hands on him at the
prompting of Holy Spirit. It was the prophecy
and vision coming to pass. Shortly after that,
he began reading a book called *Prayers that
Rout Demons* by Apostle John Eckhart. My dad
began casting out demons and doing
deliverance at his house. This is what God can
do through anyone who is willing. My dad was
what you would consider a baby Christian. He
didn't even own a Bible, but God met my dad
where his faith was and worked through him to
help my mom overcome areas of oppression.
My dad also went to a conference in 2019
called Mantles. He answered the altar call for
salvation and publicly declared his allegiance
to the Kingdom of Heaven.

"There is a time for everything, and a season
for every activity under the Heavens."

Ecclesiastes 3:1 NIV

In late 2019, I moved back in with my parents for a short time as directed by Holy Spirit. During this time, I honored my parents as much as I could, specifically by serving them. I ran errands for them such as grocery shopping, cooking, cleaning and driving them to medical appointments. I even learned how to prepare specific dishes for each of them, which was no small feat given their individually restricted dietary needs. On September 26, 2019, God sent me to another deliverance session.

This place was local to San Antonio. I had never been but had heard great things about it. After seeking Holy Spirit's guidance, I decided to make an appointment for prayer. Upon arriving, I waited for the two ladies assigned to my prayer appointment. They had spent three days praying and fasting, seeking God's will for me. One lady would ask me questions and I would respond with what I felt I was hearing from God. The second lady served as a witness to record on paper what was happening.

During the prayer session, a generational yoke manifested. It was the "monkey on my back" that kept me in emotional bondage to my dad. In the spirit, I could see that it was located at the back of my neck, similar to where a yoke would be placed on a work animal. This type of yoke is a wooden beam, sometimes fixed between a pair of animals such as oxen. It allows them to bear the load of anything they are pulling while working together. Some yokes can also be fitted to an individual animal, such as a donkey or horse. Symbolically, the yoke implies striving, inferiority, burdens and oppressions. If you have ever wondered why an abused person continuously returns to their abuser, spiritually speaking, it can be explained as a negative soul tie or a yoke. They are tied together in the spirit, and breaking or severing the tie in the natural cannot be done until it is addressed in the spirit.

"It is good for a man to bear The yoke in his youth."

Lamentations 3:27 NKJV

"For now I will break off his yoke from you, and burst your bonds apart."

Nahum 1:13 NKJV

"Take My yoke upon you and learn from Me, for I am gentle and lowly in heart, and you will find rest for your souls. For My yoke is easy and My burden is light."

Matthew 11:29-30 NKJV

As I was seeing in the spirit realm, I saw the demon trying to resist being cast out. It was similar looking to a gremlin. It was black and had a putrid smell to it. As I relayed this information to the lady facilitating deliverance of the yoke, she identified that it had been with me since childhood and was therefore, deeply rooted. She told me that Holy Spirit revealed to her that I had not been able to free myself from this particular demon in any of my self-deliverances because I couldn't recognize it. It had become so deeply rooted that I didn't distinguish where it ended and began. She continued praying and asked me if I knew what the open door was.

Throughout all this, I was experiencing such intense emotions of anger that I couldn't discern the root of this demon. The deliverance minister then told the demon to identify itself. I suddenly saw "REJECTION" in huge black letters in the spirit. I relayed this to the deliverance minister. She began to guide me through releasing the rejection in the following manner as guided by Holy Spirit:

"April, imagine a balloon with the word 'rejection' on it. It is tied to a string full of memories. Now imagine that balloon represents all the unforgiveness you have towards being rejected by your father. Focus all those emotions into the balloon and watch it grow. When you feel as though all the negative emotions are in the balloon, let go of the string of memories tied to it and let it all float away."

When I saw this happening in the spirit, the gremlin demon suddenly reached out and grabbed the string of the gray balloon. I started crying. I told the deliverance minister what was happening. Part of its body was sticking out of my neck and it was fiercely fighting to keep the balloon from floating away. I was so upset because I was ready to let it all go and this demon would not allow the rejection to leave me. This is one way that demons work against us, but unfortunately, not everyone can see when this is actually happening in the spirit realm.

The deliverance minister continued to exercise her authority telling the demon to leave. I eventually saw the gremlin-looking demon leave my neck entirely as it held on to the balloon that began to float away. Once the demon was gone, the balloon turned to a gold color and popped. It rained down golden coins. I also threw up.

"Stand fast therefore in the liberty by which Christ has made us free, and do not be entangled again with a yoke of bondage."
Galatians 5:1 NKJV

I went home after the deliverance and told my dad all about what I had experienced. He started to get offended at the thought of his behavior being linked to this demonic oppression called a yoke. He began to demonstrate accusatory behavior, at which point I felt anger rise up. Almost as soon as I felt that anger rise up, I felt joy. And then, I burst out laughing. I was laughing so hard and so loudly, my dad started laughing. Offense left the building. In that moment, the joy of the Lord was my strength. (Nehemiah 8:10 NKJV)

I truly believe this particular deliverance was made possible because I honored both my parents for a season. It was not easy to do, but it was necessary. I chose to forgive the offenses and honor my parents.

"Honor your father and your mother, that your days may be long upon the land which the Lord your God is giving you."

Exodus 20:12 NKJV

Forgiveness is a monetary transaction in the spirit. This is why I saw the golden coins showering upon me after I released the rejection and all the negative feelings associated with it. This can be found in Luke.

"'There was a certain creditor who had two debtors. One owed five hundred denarii, and the other fifty. And when they had nothing with which to repay, he freely forgave them both. Tell Me, therefore, which of them will love him more?' Simon answered and said, 'I suppose the one whom he forgave more.' And He said to him, 'You have rightly judged.'"

Luke 7:41-43 NKJV

Although it is a parable Jesus was using to teach Simon a lesson about why a sinful woman should be forgiven, we can also see the monetary transaction as it relates to forgiveness. This is a huge spiritual perk to healing from offense.

Another thing we can do is ask God to heal our memories. He can do this because He exists outside of space and time. I once asked Him to help me understand and conceptualize this. He gave me the following vision:

I saw God sitting in the middle of a circular train track. I could only see the back of Him. I instinctively knew the track represented time and the train represented my life. At first, I thought the circle meant that time at one point had been infinite.

While the train was still moving, God took the track apart and created a beginning and an end. The train represented points in my life. Each railcar was a particular moment of my life and God could stop the train from moving at any point along the tracks. He could see my life from the beginning to end. He showed me the end of the train, but not the end of the tracks.

He then showed me Jesus moving from railcar to railcar. Jesus was redeeming my past by visiting particular cars. At that moment, I knew that all I had to do was ask Jesus to redeem different areas of my life. He then showed me Jesus sitting alongside the train as it was stopped on the track. He was at the beginning, middle and end of my train all at the same time. He existed in every area of my life, and I could see how my future would literally change my past. It is a very strange concept to explain, but I was able to understand clearly how this worked.

When I understood the revelation, God showed me another railcar. It was my parents' railcar in their marriage. I could see that it carried loads and loads of generational baggage, and the railcar then rammed into my train repeatedly. My past was being redeemed by Jesus, but I needed Him to break the generational curses. When I got that revelation, God put my parents' marriage railcar on another track. It was no longer ramming my train.

When I think of this vision, the part that sticks out to me the most is God sitting in the center of the track. It's as if time was meant to be infinite, but then I realized that sin had changed this fact.

God can and will revisit the traumatic times in our lives and heal those memories. He did it for me. He doesn't show favoritism or partiality. What He does for one, He will do for all.

"Then Peter opened his mouth, and said, Of a truth I perceive that God is no respecter of persons:"

Acts 10:34 KJV

God wipes our sins away and makes our souls as white as snow.

"Come now, and let us reason together, saith the Lord: though your sins be as scarlet, they shall be as white as snow; though they be red like crimson, they shall be as wool."

Isaiah 1:18 KJV

He doesn't remember our sins because He wipes them away. When I asked God about this scripture, He showed me how healing from our pasts actually removes the sins from our pasts. It can be like it never happened once we are completely healed. I am not any of those things I did in my past because God healed me. I have the scars, but the memories are no longer a hiding place for demons.

When you have areas of unhealed trauma in your life, demons can hold on to those memories and hide in them. An example of this is the yoke I had and the gremlin demon trying to hang on to the balloon full of rejection. The rejection was tied to memories represented by the string. Once I was healed from those memories, the yoke broke and the demon could no longer hide.

Chapter 12

God's Purpose

Since the day I was delivered from the occult, God used me to baptize both my parents and several friends in the Holy Spirit. I've given myself to be an empty vessel to be used in helping deliver several people from oppressive spirits. He gives me dreams, mostly of warnings before attacks from the enemy arise so I can pray against them. He gives me open visions of angels, closed visions of the Heavens and angelic armies at war with the demonic. It has been an amazing time.

My husband, who completely disregarded all aspects of the supernatural, both good and bad, started attending church consistently. When his job changed and he couldn't attend church in person, he started watching services online. When I divinely lost my job (as God willed it), my husband said we would continue to tithe off the portion of my lost wages. His faith walk is different than mine, but he grows daily in his convictions.

I belonged to a weekly Bible study full of women in Christ who are HUNGRY for truth and knowledge. At one point, I opened up my home to host a Bible study. I began to see heavenly portals opening and closing in my house after I would bow down before the throne of God and praise Him in all His majesty. I also began to break generational curses in my family one after another. I confronted my dad about the abuse I suffered as a child, he admitted it, and apologized.

My mom's health, which was in need of a major overhaul, was completely restored. God prompted me to lay hands on her and anoint her with oil. After that, my mom ended up in the intensive care unit for three weeks and her doctors couldn't figure out what was going on. The doctors said her kidneys were in complete, irreversible damage. Slowly but surely, she improved. The doctors took her off all the medications she had been on and her test results came back with positive reports. Everything the enemy stole, he was paying back. The doctors never knew what was wrong, but she is now healthy and strong.

"Yet when he is found, he must restore sevenfold; He may have to give up all the substance of his house."

Proverbs 6:31 NKJV

Remember that angel I told you I encountered when I was three? It was a demonic angel. It brought depression into my life at three-years old and stuck with me until 2018 when I got delivered. I still experience depression when the weather is overcast, but I don't battle with it. The same is true regarding anxiety; I used to have panic attacks in the middle of rush hour traffic. I used to break down at the grocery store when I couldn't find an item I needed. Now, I get anxiety with hormonal fluctuations or when I eat certain foods, but it isn't so intense that it keeps me isolated from society and completely debilitated.

"Anxiety in the heart of man causes depression, But a good word makes it glad."

Proverbs 12:25 NKJV

How do we know when depression, anxiety, fear or whatever other issues that we struggle with are demonic? I believe Isaiah Saldivar said it best. He said, "When you can't medicate or counsel it away, it's usually demonic." For twenty years, I tried everything I knew to do to overcome depression and anxiety. When we've exhausted all our options and the treatment is only a temporary fix, that is a good indication of demonic bondage in an area.

The symptoms may look the same, but Holy Spirit can help you distinguish between what is demonic and what is maybe a chemical imbalance. An experienced deliverance minister can help too. They have a trained eye and know what to look for.

Where I live, there are two types of grapes that grow wild and in ample supply: mustang grapes and muscadine grapes. People will actually get into arguments over what kind of grapes you have growing on your property. The similarities are very obvious, but it's the distinction between the two that we really have to look for. When ripe for the picking, both have beautiful colors, one more red while the other is more purple. The muscadine grapes grow in larger clusters and are harvested as single berries instead of bunches. Mustang grapes grow in bunches of five or less and are harvested as such. The vines on my fence line usually have bunches of three or four.

Outwardly, they look similar and so do their leaves. On the inside, things get a little more complicated. Muscadine grapes have five seeds; mustang grapes have four seeds inside. The mustang grapes require more sugar when turned into jam or jelly because they are highly acidic as compared to the muscadine grapes. While both make excellent jams and jellies, only the muscadine is preferable in making wine because they are much sweeter. The leaves, although similar at a glance, are quite distinctive. The underside of a mustang grapevine leaf is silver, sometimes white in color. The underside of a muscadine leaf is a golden-green in color. How they ripen is also of distinction. Mustang grapes start green, turn pink and ripen into a beautiful deep purple color. Muscadines are a lighter-colored grape and ripen to a deep red. You have to search in the hidden places to find the identifiers so that you don't confuse one with the other.

This is the same thing with demonic bondage. Not everything will manifest itself. It takes a keen, trained, Spirit-filled eye to be able to identify the difference.

On May 5, 2019, I visited a church in San Antonio called The Rock. It is now known as All Nations Worship Assembly, San Antonio. I attended their anniversary service. It was packed with powerful worship, praise and warring in the spirit. I remember seeing a lot of open heavenly portals in the building. I even saw one in the restroom, which I thought was kind of incredible. At the end of the service, Apostle Kevin Duhart asked if there were any

first-time visitors at the service. When he asked
this, my spirit leapt and I let out a loud shout. It
caught his attention and he called me up to the
front of the room. I stood at the altar while he
remained on the pulpit. He asked my name
and started prophesying over me. At one point,
he said, "Now, we are going to move April into
the maternal side of her family and some of the
chaos that's been in the bloodline there. We
cut that off you now in Jesus' name. Two
generations, the grandmother, that thing she
carried, that confusion in the family, we curse it.
We command it off you now. Loose her! Let her
go; let her go!"

At this point, I was slain in the Spirit and fell to
the floor. I started laughing uncontrollably and
stayed that way for a few minutes because I
was again feeling the joy of the Spirit. I did not
immediately know what Apostle Duhart was
referring to, so I asked Holy Spirit to reveal it to
me. The next day, I had a vision of laying
hands on my grandmother who currently lives
in a nursing home. She is afflicted with

dementia, which had been the confusion and chaos he'd cast off me.

Alz.org says, "Dementia is a general term for loss of memory, language, problem-solving and other thinking abilities that are severe enough to interfere with daily life. Alzheimer's is the most common cause of dementia." NHS.uk says, "Dementia is not a disease itself. It's a collection of symptoms that result from damage to the brain caused by different diseases, such as Alzheimer's. These symptoms vary according to the part of the brain that is damaged."

Early signs of dementia include loss of memory, inability to concentrate, difficulty carrying out daily tasks due to one getting confused over the correct ingredients when cooking, difficulty remembering words, confusion regarding times or places and mood changes. It is also noted that dementia is not a natural part of aging, however, most people do associate aging with dementia.

Interestingly, these are symptoms I experienced while demonized with depression and anxiety. My focus was off, daily tasks seemed overwhelming and my moods were all over the place. Looking back, I can definitely make the connection between the demonic oppression I'd experienced at a younger age which had been diagnosed as Bipolar disorder to the symptoms one might experience with dementia. I am not a doctor and do not purport to be one, but as someone who's suffered demonic oppression for a long time, I can definitely see the similarities. This is no surprise given the fact that demons travel in packs.

As far as my grandmother was concerned, I didn't immediately understand what it was she carried because I am not close to her. Her relationship with my mom was strained while I was growing up so we didn't see much of her. It is common knowledge in my family, however, that she is currently in a nursing home and suffers from the symptoms know as dementia. When Holy Spirit reminded me of this, I realized that I'd received deliverance for something I had completely forgotten was in my bloodline.

"That servant who knows his master's will and does not get ready or does not do what his master wants will be beaten with may blows. But the one who does not know and does things deserving punishment will be beaten with few blows. From everyone who has been given much, much will be demanded; and from the one who has been entrusted with much, much more will be asked."

Luke 12:47-48 NIV

My love affair with God started the first time I felt His Glory. His love affair with me started before I was in my mother's womb. I am so humbled and thankful that God never left me or forsook me, even when my immediate family did and even when I'd turned my back on Him so much so that I'd given my life over to the enemy. Many people will not experience what I've experienced, but I'm thankful that it's all a part of my testimony.

At first, I wasn't sure why it took me almost four years to write this testimony, but now I understand why. God wanted me to be able to testify to the whole story. I am a woman redeemed by God. I am a woman impacting one person at a time. I am a woman who was touched by another fierce woman of God, and it changed my entire generational line. I am a woman maintaining my deliverance and I pray I can help others learn to do the same.

I often wonder why no one saw any red flags throughout my childhood. One of my aunts, who was Spirit-filled and is now resting in Heaven, did bring it to my parents' attention that something was wrong with me when I was about 15-years old, but my parents saw her observation as intrusive, judgmental and unwelcome. This was a spirit of accusation manifesting in my parents against my aunt. We need to be able to identify the pig no matter how much lipstick it puts on. No one saw the red flags because nothing was brought into the light. The Word brings life and healing. The truth really does set people free.

"And you shall know the truth, and the truth shall make you free."

John 8:32 NKJV

My daughters are now six-years old and almost two-years old, and I now teach them about their identity and the authority they have in Christ Jesus. When my oldest is scared, she knows how to stand against fear and tell it to leave. When she prays, she puts a demand on Heaven and the ear of God to listen. She understands the power of prayer for healing and she knows the power of her tongue.

My oldest daughter is also a seer and a discerner. She was baptized in the Holy Spirit when she was three. She asked God into her heart when she was four, and just recently, she asked to be water baptized. I am equipping her and her sister to fiercely stand against the enemy who tried to wipe out our family. She asks me often about generational curses, yokes, familiar spirits and so forth because she hears me talk about these things as I continue to heal from them. It is okay to let your children see you broken as long as you let them watch God put you back together.

"It was he who gave some to be apostles, some to be prophets, some to be evangelists, and some to be pastors and teachers, to prepare God's people for works of service, so that the body of Christ may be built up until we all reach unity in the faith and in the knowledge of the Son of God and become mature, attaining to the whole measure of the fullness of Christ."

Ephesians 4:11-13 NIV

"The mature children of God are those who are moved by the impulses of the Holy Spirlt."

Romans 8:14 TPT

The beacon of light that local church was to me when I needed it most was the Holy Spirit anointing that was on Pat. Pat takes zero credit for that day because she knows God did all the work. I am forever grateful to her heart of submission to our Lord. It has been almost four years since I was delivered from the occult. Pat closely mentored me for about six months after the initial incident, and over time, God put us on different paths. Every now and then, I reach out to Pat. I ask her about things Holy Spirit revealed to me and she gives me further insight.

One day, Pat and I went to eat and I asked her about her experience with the occult. She had done missionary work in Mexico, serving in a voluntary dental clinic for the local people. She said she and her friend were on their last patient when two witches and a warlock walked into the clinic. They were curious as to what was happening inside the clinic and had been observing the work being done. There was a young man who came in and informed Pat and her friend that he had an assignment from Satan to kill her. She told me she laughed, hoped he wouldn't be too disappointed and told him to sit and wait. They fed the young man, made him comfortable and showed him love. Pat and her friend noticed that one of his legs was shorter than the other one. She and her friend laid hands on him and commanded his leg to grow out. After witnessing that miracle, the witches told Pat they wanted to know how to do that kind of magic. She then witnessed the gospel to the three of them and they gave their lives over to Jesus. They were also delivered and set free.

Pat never experienced any backlash over my deliverance. When I asked her about that, she said, "I didn't have any backlash because I didn't give the enemy any power over me." When you plead the blood of Jesus over you, you are protected from any evil. It requires faith to believe that God is doing ALL the work. We are just empty vessels. He fills us with His powerful Holy Spirit. No weapon formed against us will prosper, but do we truly believe this, or is it just a saying? My faith is in Him alone. Staying prayed up is always important because the devil doesn't take a break. He is relentless, but do you know your identity? Do you know who you are? Knowing your identity legalizes your authority! The anointing expressed with power and authority is what defeats the enemy."

"I will sacrifice a freewill offering to You; I will praise Your name, O Lord, for it is good. For He has delivered me from all my troubles, and my eyes have looked in triumph on my foes."

Psalm 54:6-7 NIV

Relying on God is an absolute must. We should not become overly confident in our own abilities. During my trip to Belize, the divemaster often shared stories of what he'd experienced in his many years of diving. He told us of one man known on the island for skin diving. He was well-known by the locals and also left grand impressions on the tourists. "Skin diving is the action or sport of swimming underwater without a diving suit, typically in deep water using an aqualung and flippers" (Source: Oxford Languages). Our divemaster told us that this one man would often dive without any equipment other than his spear and flippers.

During one of his many regular dives, the skin diver was met with a group of scuba divers. He decided to go deep diving with them. One of the things taught in scuba diving is regulating the pressure in your lungs when coming up for dives. You do this by exhaling the air as you're ascending so that your lungs don't over-expand. The skin diver was not accustomed to this practice because he didn't normally dive deep enough to be concerned about this. When he went deep diving with the scuba divers, he surfaced too quickly. His lungs exploded and he died. In this case, he exceeded his area of expertise and it proved to be a fatal mistake.

Not all situations end fatally. God is, after all, our Redeemer. In a tiny town in Texas called Rockdale, there was this huge Alcoa aluminum plant and they had been there for 56 years. They provided forty percent of the county's taxes and 65 percent of the school district's budget. The plant drew big businesses to the town like Wal-Mart and multiple car dealerships (Source: grist.org "Life after Alcoa", 10/30/2019).

Local rumor has it that Alcoa was exposed for

leaking poison, and they had the option to clean up or to leave. They decided to leave. Eventually, they would spend twenty years cleaning up the toxic waste left behind in order to sell the site. Recently, the former site became home to the world's largest bitcoin mining operation. It's not something everyone talks about because of the stigma associated with the previous plant. Not many people know about it, and it is thriving because of the infrastructure that was already there. Now local rumor has it that the tiny town of Rockdale will soon recover from the fallout of the Alcoa debacle. This is a picture of the redemption we experience as Christians.

Chapter 13

Prayers

Over the course of the last four years, I have written several prayers to help set my family and friends free as well as maintain my deliverance and consecration. The following are some of these prayers. Personalize them for you and your family and declare the living Word of our God over your bloodline to set the captives free.

Daily Prayer Declaration of 2018

This is the day the Lord has made, I will rejoice and be glad in it! Father, thank You for sacrificing Your only Son. Thank You for the blank sheet of paper, white as snow, covered by the blood of Jesus. Jesus, thank You for willingly being led like a lamb to slaughter for my salvation. Holy Spirit, thank You for being

with and in me, guiding me, and comforting
me. Let my thoughts, my words, and my
actions be Your thoughts, Your words, and Your
actions. I bless You, praise You, honor You and
glorify You. Let my life be a free will offering to
You. I pray for Your sovereign will, Your moral
will and Your personal will in my life. In Jesus'
name. Amen.

Prayer Over Family Bound By the Occult

In Jesus' name, I pray against all spirits of
witchcraft, religion, perversion, ancestral
curses, vows, and practices known or unknown
in this house. I come against the spirit of
deception and call down God's holy hand of
protection on this household. I thank God for
His sovereign will and dominion over all things
of this existence, including heavenly and
otherworldly angels/demons/spirits. I thank
God that the struggle we fight is not against
flesh and blood, but is against the rulers,
against the authorities, against the powers of
this dark world, and against the spiritual forces

of evil in the heavenly realms (Ephesians 6:12).

Romans 8:11 says if the Spirit of Him who raised Jesus from the dead is living in you, He who raised Christ from the dead will also give life to your mortal bodies through His Spirit, who lives in you. We stand on this resurrection power within us that has been granted to us by God Himself against enemies of God's holy throne.

Romans 8:15 says that we did not receive a spirit that makes us a slave again to fear, but we received the Spirit of sonship. It is on God's Word and authority that we stand against fear and evil. The Bible says that whatever is bound on Earth is bound in Heaven and that which is loosed on Earth is loosed in Heaven. By God's authority, I bind the spirit of the occult and every demon in its network that has oppressed and possessed my family. I ask for God's heavenly legion of angels to act on our behalf to engage in spiritual warfare in the heavenly realms against these demons of oppression.

I ask for God to keep His Word, according to Ezekiel 36:26, for my family, which says that God will give them new hearts and put a new spirit in them; that God will remove their hearts of stone and give them hearts of flesh. And that God will put His Spirit in them and move them to follow His decrees so that they will be careful to keep His laws.

According to Ezekiel 37:1-6, I pray that God will speak to my family's dry bones and put breath in them. I pray that He will cause them to come to life so they will know that God is the Lord!

I believe in the power and Word of my Lord and Savior, Jesus Christ, and stand in agreement with these words as I pray for the deliverance and salvation of my family. I stand in the gap on behalf of my family and ask God to reveal Himself to them in a powerful, chain-breaking way. I ask for God to have mercy on my family and withhold any judicial hardening of their hearts. In Jesus' name. Amen!

Holy Spirit Inspired Declaration

In the name of Jesus, I break the assignment, attachment, attack, and perversion associated with parasitical and negative impartations in my life, both generationally and those that were spoken over me. I command an immediate halt to all negative, generational impartations and curses in my bloodline, and I forbid them from taking root or having fruit in my life, the lives of my children and the lives of my family. I ask God's angels to dry up the burrowed and ungodly roots in my life and replace them with the fruits of the Spirit. I expose all negative impartations in my life with the light of the Word. I disclose my dedication to God so that His secrets will dwell within me to be made known in His timing. Everyone I come into contact with cannot help but feel the favor and grace of God upon my life because I am a freewill sacrifice, burning up the demonic spirits daily. My fuel is the Holy Spirit within me. My breath is the blood of Jesus. My directives come to me from the Word of God. My presence brings forth the Fire of God. My children are blessings to all who they come in contact with. Their laughter is supernaturally anointed with the Spirit of Joy. Their smiles bring immediate peace. Their hugs project nothing but love. All automobiles in my possession are chariots unto the Lord. Everywhere I drive is automatically claimed as territory for the Kingdom of God. The exhaust of my vehicles does not pollute the Earth, but brings healing to the land. Every place my feet tread becomes holy ground for God. Demonic spirits cannot stay when I show up. I don't have to speak it because I breathe it. I command atmospheric change by God's will. I belong everywhere I go. I am purposed by God's will. I walk in fellowship with angels on assignment for God's will. My anointing increases exponentially each day by God's will. Glory to glory will know no limits in my life. I sing God's praises in my sleep. My presence binds the transmission and communication of demonic information in those around me. I send confusion into the enemy's camp. I cause demons to flee because of God within me. My hedge of protection is impenetrable to demonic forces. I exercise supernatural power and

authority because I am a child of God. In
Jesus' name. Amen.

Identity Declaration

I am a child of the Most High. I am the apple of
God's eye. I carry forth God's will. I am wholly
submitted to the lordship of the Ancient of
Days. I pray for God's will in my life and the
lives of my family. I expect God's will to be
done without fail, limitations or hesitation. I
decree and declare that nothing can stop the
Hand of God from moving on Earth as it is in
Heaven. I am a supernatural being made in the
image of my supernatural God. I walk in the
supernatural love, favor and blessings of my
Lord. I have unending grace and mercy
renewed daily. I am who God created me to be.
I am nothing without God. I know these things,
therefore I know I am a Glory carrier by God's
will. I cast out demons. I heal the sick. I
operate in miracles, signs and wonders. I raise
the dead. I prophesy accurately by God's will. I
speak by God's voice. I pray God's will. I
intercede like Jesus. I command God's will to

be done. I manifest God's will on Earth. I do not live in regret, second guessing or doubt. I know my destiny in God is purposely and divinely ordered. I am not double-minded. I am rooted in the foundation of God alone. I love my Lord and Savior above all else. I worship my King of Kings. I cannot be shaken. I hear God's voice. I crave Holy Spirit's presence in my life. I encounter God daily. I rest in God's presence. I dwell in God's presence. I live for God alone. I do not seek approval from man, but from God. I am not bound or oppressed. I discern by the guidance of Holy Spirit. I receive wisdom and knowledge from Holy Spirit. I give all praise, honor and glory to my God, the Father, Jesus of Nazareth, the Son and Holy Spirit. I openly live my life in submission to God. I will continually seek God's will in my life and for my life. I will continually ask for revelation. I cannot be squashed by the enemy. I squash the enemy. God's power is alive in me because I die to myself daily. I am reliant on God alone. I will not grieve Holy Spirit or quench Him. I give way to God's will in my life. I am marked for the Kingdom of Heaven. I am chosen. I am loved. I work in partnership with angels for God's will alone. Angels encamp around, guard, and help me because I am God's favored. I am protected. I am hedged. I was blind, but now I see. I ask, seek and knock with expectation. I raise Holy children for God's Kingdom. My children will have an ever-increasing portion of my blessings. I speak, breathe, live and will live forever in God's manifested Word. In Jesus' name, I pray. Because God hears the prayers of a righteous woman, it is done. Amen.

Prayer Declaration for My Children

In the name of Jesus, I speak God's blessings and impartations over my children and all future generations. The callings on their lives cannot be broken, silenced, impeded, blocked, hindered, muted or canceled. I decree and declare God's favor will be continually released upon my children for God's will. They will not know the struggles or curses I have known because they are highly favored and blessed. I plead the blood of Jesus over their lives and I declare that His blood lives in their veins. I pronounce and announce that holy and supernatural expectations and experiences will be normal in their lives. My children are not only claimed for the Kingdom, they rule with the Father in the Kingdom. My children are warriors for the Kingdom. They will not have the fear of man binding their minds, will, actions or emotions. My children will know their God, His will for their lives and how to work on assignments with their angels. The spirit of backslide cannot manifest in their lives. Open doors to the demonic are hereby shut, locked, chained and God's angels are standing guard to keep them closed. Angels minister to my children 24/7 by God's will. God Himself ministers to my children. Rejection, offense and oppression cannot manifest in my children's lives. I speak a multiplication of the fruit of the Spirit to bind, block and annihilate any demonic spirits. I do not quench my children's gifts. I encourage their callings. I raise them up in God's Word. I bless them under God and above all negativity. My children's innocence will not be perverted. Their innocence is guarded by the fire of God. Restoration and renewal of their minds, bodies and souls will be continually springing forth because the living waters of God flows through them. My children will exercise their power and authority by God's grace and mercy in their lives. My children know God so well that when they encounter the enemy, they will not be shaken. My children will thirst and hunger for God in a way that God Himself has never experienced. My children will call down the Kingdom of Heaven daily. No harm shall befall my children as they war with the enemies of darkness because God has gone before them and directed their steps. Darkness will tremble when my children pray. My children will know financial stability, blessings and favor. My children will know the blessings of Jabez all their lives. My children will not know lack, but they will know humility in Christ. My children will be a blessing to others. My children will honor their mother and father that it may go well with them. My children are supernaturally and intellectually empowered by God. My children cannot be overtaken or overcome. Favor will chase my children all the days of their lives. Hallelujah! In Jesus' name. Amen.

Prayer of Repentance

Father, I confess my actions and I thank You for receiving my repentance so I may receive Your forgiveness. I reject and break agreement with any spirits that may have entered through my eyes or ears. I break agreement with ANY spirits that are not of God in the name of Jesus. You are not welcome here with me, my family or in my house. I thank God for the blood of Jesus over myself and my family. I thank God for Psalm 91 that no pestilence will come near my household. Anything that is here that is not of God has to go now, in the name of Jesus. Amen.

Love Declaration

"Love suffers long and is kind; love does not envy; love does not parade itself, is not puffed up; does not behave rudely, does not seek its own, is not provoked, thinks no evil; does not

rejoice in iniquity, but rejoices in the truth;
bears all things, believes all things, hopes all
things, endures all things."

I Corinthians 13:4-7 NKJV

I suffer long and am kind; I do not envy, I do
not parade myself, I am not puffed up; I do not
behave rudely, I do not seek my own, I am not
provoked, I think no evil; I do not rejoice in
iniquity but I rejoice in the truth; I bear all
things, believe God in all things, hope all things
and I endure all things. In Jesus' name. Amen.

The Prayer of Jabez

"And Jabez called on the God of Israel saying,
"Oh, that You would bless me indeed, and
enlarge my territory, that Your hand would be
with me, and that You would keep me from evil,
that I may not cause pain!" So God granted
him what he requested."

I Chronicles 4:10 NKJV

Father, bless me indeed. Enlarge my territory,
keep Your hand upon me and keep me from

evil so that I may not cause pain to myself or others. I ask this for my house and my family, in the name of Jesus.

There are several books on this powerful prayer. I recommend "The Prayer of Jabez: Breaking Through to the Blessed Life" by Bruce H. Wilkinson.

Chapter 14

Eyewitness Testimony

Pat has willingly offered to provide her account of what she witnessed when I manifested. Here is her recollection of what happened:

"My name is Pat Mendoza and my husband is David Mendoza. We were both ministering the night April approached us. My husband and I are always ready for anything that comes our way. Demonic spirits have assignments; they have been instructed to kill, steal or destroy, but Jesus has come that they may have life, and have it to the fullest (John 10:10).

April was desperate that night. My heart went out to her because I could feel her pain. I clearly remember the tone in her voice. I knew it was not her speaking. April had her battles I could sense that night, but I knew that the Lord was not going to send her home the same way she came in. When I gave April my phone number, I knew that the assignment was not over. Going to her house the next day to pray over her home was the next step. Once she was delivered, I followed up by praying over their home. Holy Spirit leads us in all truths. Being prayed up is important at all times because you never know who you are going to be praying for.

A group of ushers who were serving that evening surrounded us. These men were instructed to pray in the Holy Spirit and to not get close to April. The look in the ushers' eyes was clearly an indication that they had never seen anything like this before. Once we finished praying for April and seeing the difference in her demeanor, the ushers were astonished at what the Lord had done.

I have been on multiple mission trips to Mexico where you see great manifestations. It is vital that when you go out into the world, you must stay prayed up. When you encounter people who are demonized, you must be ready to set them free. We have the power and authority that God has given us.

"Look, I have given you authority over all the power of the enemy, and you can walk among snakes and scorpions and crush them. Nothing will injure you."

Luke 10:19 NLT

There were many instances that people would lay hands on the demonized individual and the person praying would start to throw up black tar, get severe headaches and begin to be tortured. You must have a partner to pray with you and have faith to believe that God does all the work.

"Heal the sick, raise the dead, cure those with leprosy, and cast out demons. Give as freely as you have received!"

Matthew 10:8 NLT

I am very proud of April for her testimony. April has an assignment to set people free. This book will set people free and give them hope that God is real. He makes a way when there seems to be no way (Isaiah 43:16). Her bravery is evident in the fact that she's willing to speak about a subject that many do not want to touch.

"The Spirit of the Sovereign Lord is on me, because the Lord has anointed me to proclaim good news to the poor. He has sent me to bind up the brokenhearted, to proclaim freedom for the captives and release from darkness for the prisoners, to proclaim the year of the Lord's favor and the day of vengeance of our God, to comfort all who mourn."

Isaiah 61:1-2 NIV